Acclaim for *The Personal Success Handbook*

"I love books that make a difference – and *The Personal Success Handbook* is one of those! Packed full of useful ideas, it gives direction and a sense of purpose as you read it. It focuses attention on the practical and possible action steps needed to move anyone's life forward in all areas. The illustrative stories add to our understanding and the many exercises and activities woven throughout the text, encourage us gently, but firmly, along the path of change. Easy to read, free of jargon, thought provoking and purposeful – a book for those people serious about life improvement – so LET'S DO IT!"
– ***Gill Fielding***, The Wealth Company (The Secret Millionaire, Channel 4)

" CurlyMartin tops off a terrific trilogy in her 'handbook' series with an intensive examination of the multi-faceted and elusive gem we know as personal success.

Here we are not only introduced to a whole host of subjects that can enhance our lives, but are treated to Curly's very own RAWPOWER model, borne from over two decades of her own personal success. I found this to be a highly useful tool that I could apply instantly to my life to help expedite success.

The Personal Success Handbook is written in Curly's warm and absorbing style once again, which makes the subject matter breathe with her fresh perspective and delightful humour. It offers the reader plenty of opportunity to reflect on what is being presented, as well as encouragement to take action to move us forward on our journey to success – something not always present in books of this nature.

Quite simply put, this book would be outstanding addition to the library of anyone who is serious about personal development; whatever your current level of achievement, the *Personal Success Handbook* will help propel you off the starting blocks down the track to YOUR personal success with a renewed perspective and inspired confidence."
– ***Grant Willcox*** – Success Coach – 2Excel Coaching

"One of Curly's many strengths is her ability to put across (complicated) information in an easy to understand manner. Having met Curly various times I can wholeheartedly say that she is a living and breathing example of her methodologies. Her first two books were great; this is even better. *The Personal Success Handbook* is fun, informative and potentially life-changing"
– *Joe Benitez*, IKEA Business Manager (UK)

"This superb practical book starts by asking you to define what success means for you. Once that is decided you can select topics ranging from health, finances, spiritual, emotional control, career planning, getting the ideal job, easy to use models for influencing your boss and relationships. All chapters have stories for each area and soul searching questions to guide you towards attaining your success. No hype, just great easy to use ideas and strategies so that you can get out of bed on a wet Monday morning with a smile on your face!"
– *Zoë Fakouri* LLM, MCIPS.

"Curly Martin has a unique talent to take what is good and make it even better. *The Personal Success Handbook* is an extension of Curly's insightful expertise and wisdom in self-development. If you have not been lucky enough to attend one of her courses or hear her speak in public, this is the next best thing. Since working with Curly I have built a thriving business and a wonderful reputation as both a coach and therapist, earning me a place in The Daily Telegraph's Top 20 Health Gurus in 2007. I owe much of my success to Curly's invaluable knowledge and motivation."
– *Chris Smith* – Professional Coach, NLP Practitioner and Hypnotherapist

"I have been studying personal development for over 20 years and when I picked up the *Personal Success Handbook* I thought it would just be re-iterating what I had already covered. I was pleasantly surprised that the approach of the book is different to many that I have read. It contains aspects that I had not previously covered. When I find myself now incorporating things that I learned in this book, I smile. I also get the desired results! Thank you Curly for another great book.
– *Ric Hayman* – Performance Coach, Hypnotherapist and EFT Trainer

The Personal Success Handbook

Curly Martin

Crown House Publishing Limited
www.crownhouse.co.uk
www.chpus.com

First published by

Crown House Publishing Ltd
Crown Buildings, Bancyfelin, Carmarthen, Wales, SA33 5ND, UK
www.crownhouse.co.uk

and

Crown House Publishing Company LLC
6 Trowbridge Drive, Suite 5, Bethel, CT 06801-2858, USA
www.CHPUS.com

British Library Cataloguing-in-Publication Data
A catalogue entry for this book is available
from the British Library.

13 Digit ISBN 978-184590090-8

LCCN 2007938980

All stories in this book are true but the names of the individuals
concerned have been changed

Printed and bound in the UK by
Cromwell Press, Trowbridge, Wiltshire

To the memory of my father
Frank Glanville James Martin.

Author Profile

In 1992, Curly Martin was diagnosed with breast cancer, which had mutated into an aggressive form of lymphatic cancer and she was given nine months to live. At that time she became homeless and was unemployed. Since then she has become the bestselling author of *The Handbook Series*; she is a highly sought-after international speaker, a pioneer of life coaching in Europe and the founder of a very successful coaching company, Achievement Specialists Limited.

In this, the third book of the series, she intuitively combines her personal experiences with accepted methodologies and cutting-edge innovations to create exciting, entertaining and effective approaches to personal success and development. She shows you how you too can become successful using the RAWPOWER strategy she used to turn her life around.

She shares with you all the knowledge, tips and secrets she has discovered during her 20-plus years in senior management positions within global corporations. In this book you will find the techniques and strategies she used to overcome her physical challenges and how she now lives a passionate, exciting, wealthy, healthy, happy and spiritual life.

Curly would love to hear from you, so visit her websites to support your journey through this book www.achievementspecialists.co.uk and www.curlymartin.com where you can read some of the testimonials from her many clients and even become one yourself.

Table of Contents

Acknowledgements

My outstanding team including Chris Smith, Ric Hayman, Margaret Edmonson and Veronica Cooper for all the support, laughs and challenges you have given me along the way.

Jackie Fletcher for her amazing proofreading expertise and for the many funny comments in the margins of the manuscript, which always made me laugh out loud. Colin Edwards for all his literary advice, wizardry and late-night editing, which provided the means for this work to get to the publishers within the very tight deadline. Mary Edwards, yet again, for her support of Colin.

Muriel Martin, Mary and Pat McEntee, Muriel and Roger Walters, the rest of my family and my loyal friends, who understood that I could not come out to play while managing a successful business and writing a book simultaneously.

To Keith Down who has always been there for me. The Bidlake bunch for the many diverting hours spent around the kitchen table. Dr Fiasal Samji, who saved my life and Anne Williams who taught me how to perform lymphatic drainage on my right arm so that I can write; both of whom made the recovery from breast and lymphatic cancer, a rewarding journey.

My husband, Pete, for his love, support and for regularly reminding me to go and run along the beautiful Bournemouth beach, which kept me focused and fit.

For all the wonderful people who have trusted me to train them to become outstanding coaches, who are now running their own successful businesses. To my team of mentor coaches who unreservedly give of their knowledge and experience to our new fledgling coaches, you can see them by visiting *Our Coaches* page on my website: www.achievementspecialists.co.uk.

Finally, for the team at Crown House who work hard to support their authors and who had faith in my first book, *The Life Coaching*

Handbook, and again for my second book, *The Business Coaching Handbook.*

Introduction

Some personal notes from Curly Martin

This introduction is a vital part of the book.

Even if you typically skip pages like this, now is a great time to change the habits of a lifetime, because you are about to discover strategies that can deliver success in any area of your life. This introduction will help you to get the optimum benefits from the ideas and concepts that follow, so stay with it for a few moments longer.

The fun begins

This book is for you if you are ready to make changes in your life, to define success on your own terms, and to take the actions that can bring it about. You deserve the life that you desire rather than the life that you have been given.

Your focus and needs will change as you change and evolve, so remember to revisit the chapter summaries from time to time as some ideas will become more meaningful to you when you begin to create positive results.

It can be infuriating to read about a good idea and then be unable to find it again later, so I invite you to personalise your book by making margin notes that apply to your life. Put a date on each note so that you can monitor how your thoughts change. Keep a pen handy as you read so that you can circle your significant page numbers as an additional rapid reference guide.

Ideas for success will come to you as you read and may well be forgotten by the time you turn the page. Ideas are as fragile as wispy white clouds which can appear on a beautiful summer day, and vanish almost as soon as you can say 'look at that beautiful cloud'. Any one of your ideas could be a breakthrough moment of 'Aha!' brilliance that can ignite your imagination. Use a small notebook to capture key word reminders of your ideas as they come to you and then refer to them later when you have more time to develop them into actions.

You will find several text boxes that are designed to make you think about your personal success and prompt you to consider how you will improve it. Spend time with the questions and write down your answers as you go along.

The boxes are deliberately small because they should work as reminders and motivators. Make more detailed observations in your notebook as soon as ideas are generated, as this will strengthen your commitments and act as your silent coach. There, I have said it, that magic word 'coach'. Coaching may not be magic, but the outcomes it can create may seem nothing less than magical.

You will probably have come across coaching in a sporting context. Success coaching works just as effectively in every area of your life. Self-analysis without a support system can be difficult and demoralising. You can only start on a journey from where you are now and your journey to personal success follows this rule. Similarly, you must have a defined destination in mind otherwise you will drift off course and, even worse, will not know when you have arrived!

Whether you opt for self-coaching or invite external help, it is all about knowing where you are, where you are going and the actions that you will take to get there. Coaching is not a quick fix; it is a process that provides a constant and continuous drip-feeding of information to fuel your motivation, to plan and make any changes that are needed, and to keep you on track by making the most of what you have.

Please set aside at least five minutes each day to spend time with this book, your notebook and pen. Plan and write down the actions you will take—no matter how small the steps may seem, they will lead you towards your goals, aims and success objectives.

If you keep doing the same things in the same ways, you will always achieve the same results. If those results correspond exactly to your definition of success, then congratulations. If not, then the following chapters offer you a series of signposts to point you in the right direction of change.

Effective coaching uses metaphors, examples and analogies to deliver results. That is why you will find a brief real-life story to launch each chapter. As they say in some movies, 'The stories are true, only the identities have been changed to protect the innocent.'

Are you ready to start writing and living your own story? It has a three-word title: *My Successful Life*. I want you to share a system that I have been using for a long time and which I created as a quick reminder/reference guide to inspire me to greater achievements.

Each time I unearth a new or unexplored area I apply a system I call the RAWPOWER model to accelerate my development in that area. As you check it out now, and when you use it later, consider how it applies to your own current success and future success progress.

R – Read as much as I can on the subject
A   – Attend seminars, courses, talks, demonstrations etc.
W   – Watch audio visual materials on the area
P   – Personal insights that apply to me
O   – Open my mind when I approach the topic
W   – Work on my weaknesses in this and related areas
E   – Enjoy what I am doing
R   – Reproduce consistently high results

Due diligence

You will probably come across 'due diligence' sooner rather than later in your life. It is often stated as the slightly odd sounding, 'doing due diligence'.

This is what all buyers should do before agreeing to any transaction, whether they are buying a book, a car or even a company. In plain language, you 'do due diligence' when you flick through the pages in a bookstore, when you take a test drive or when you examine a company's financial records. What you are doing is satisfying yourself that the objects of your desire meet your needs, are fit for the purpose and represent good value.

Guess who this responsibility is down to? You may seek the advice of people who should know, you may include personal recommendations in your decision, but ultimately the buck stops with you. You take responsibility for your actions, fully and totally.

It is sometimes claimed that we live in a society of blame culture. As far as your success is concerned, forget about blame. Your life is down to you alone. All the decisions you make are down to you alone. And guess who is going to apply the principles, tips and hints in this book?

Remember this saying: 'If it is to be, it is up to me!' This is especially true about creating your personal success. This book will help you, and if you support your efforts using my RAWPOWER model your success will arrive more quickly than you could have imagined.

All this information is based on my own 20-plus years of practical experience as a coach and is presented with tremendous goodwill. I am the founder of a very successful coaching and coach-training business, which has been operating successfully for over ten years. I am not a lawyer, an accountant or a medical person. You need to know this because in legal, financial and health matters you *must* always seek the services of appropriately trained and qualified professionals as part of your personal due diligence. Because I have no control over the way that you use the information in these pages, your due diligence must also recognise that you alone are responsible for compliance with local rules and regulations, with governmental obligations and, equally importantly, for the outcomes of any actions that you take. This book is a valuable guide, and remember, the responsibility for the way that you apply its ideas to achieve success is yours!

A special bonus

When you have read this book and applied the ideas and suggestions in each chapter, you may still feel that your circumstances could benefit from the personal input of a professional coach working with you in a one-on-one session. As a special bonus, you can email your contact details (in absolute commercial confidence) to Achievement Specialists and a member of our coaching team will reply with a time and date for an introductory chat, which will be free of cost or obligation. This added benefit alone could be worth far more than the cover price of your book!

You will find our e-mail address at the end of the book. After all, you really should read everything else first!

You are about to be reminded of things that you already know and also some things that are new to you. Just because we know how to do something, it does not follow that we do it.
So ask yourself regularly:
'Am I doing what I know I need to do today?'

Chapter One

Success Defined

Success means different things to different people.

Synopsis

This chapter invites you to define what success means to you, looks at some of the ingredients for success in any arena and offers valuable tools for refining your own definition.

Anthony and Dominic had been friends for almost as long as they could remember. They met when they sat together on their first day at infants' school. Each was made welcome as part of the family in the other's house. They played together and studied together and later went out with girls together. Then, as is the way of the world, their paths diverged in adulthood although they remained best friends.

Anthony was always the more adventurous of the two so, when he left school and became, in the words of a tutor, a 'perpetual trainee', his peers were not surprised. He trained as a rubber planter in Malaysia, as a fisherman in Trinidad, as a tour guide in Marrakech and as a management consultant in Slough. When a shotgun wedding was announced, and when his son was born six months later, it was not a shock. He started his own consultancy practice from a spare bedroom and appeared to have achieved success. He just said that each of his trainee days had been a success too—'the most valuable universities ever,' he claimed.

Dominic was more studious and reserved. He did a degree course and was accepted as a junior in the civil service. His dedication and strong work ethic were eventually recognised and rewarded with progressive promotions although these did not happen as quickly as he would have liked. He never married because his few girlfriends found him a bit of a geek who had no interests outside work but still, he was happy and diligently recorded each promotion in his diary as another success step. Eventually, he inherited his parents' house, the one where he had been born and where he lived until his death.

At Dominic's packed funeral, Anthony was the obvious candidate to deliver the eulogy. He listed Dom's attributes and achievements, which Dominic's many friends had supplied him with, sincerely and with true praise as he revealed that his friend had achieved a truly enviable success because, 'He was a good man who made a positive impact on the lives of all who knew him.'

By this time, Anthony had formed his fifth company having sold two at a profit, run two into the ground and gone bankrupt with the other. He and his third wife, an eye-candy trophy, left the church together in his black-and-chromed Chrysler convertible. They set off to look for a new house. It would be the tenth that he had lived in.

Dominic, the plodder, had achieved success in his own terms and in the eyes of his employers who sent along the pension-fund manager to pay their respects. Anthony freely admitted to anyone who would listen that his life had been a roller-coaster ride of extreme highs and lows. He had impacted on many people in his turbulent wake. He was a self-made man and led a successful life of a very different kind. As he told his latest wife when they first met, 'My life has been fun and that, to me, is the ultimate definition of success.'

Seven billion definitions, but only one for you

It should be easy to define success. All you have to do is look it up in a dictionary. But this book is not just about success, it is about *personal success*, which makes the task slightly more complicated.

As I write these words it is estimated that the total population of the world is around 6.7 billion souls—and increasing year on year. It thus follows that there are potentially almost 7 billion definitions of personal success, simply because each individual will have their own idea of what it means to them.

As this is a 'handbook', we need to discover ways of cutting that enormous wealth of definitions down to a manageable level. From my dimly remembered physics lessons, if you repeat a distillation process you will finally be left with a concentrated version of whatever you started with. So that is what we will do in this chapter; we will end up with a powerful essence of success definitions which will contain all the elements but is still uniquely and personally yours.

About now you may be wondering why we would want to bother. Well, I am assuming that you want or desire success which is why you chose this book in the first place. The very first step in acquiring what you want is to know what you want. That one word, 'success', is too vague as an answer. To set out on a non-specific quest is like a child who says, 'I want to be famous' but who has no answer about how or why they could achieve fame. Neither success nor fame is found in vagueness.

Here you will be shown how to flesh out your notion of personal success and I will offer you a generic definition of my own. But first, supposing I told you that there is no such thing as success or its equal and opposite force, failure?

What I mean is that these do not exist in the sense that you can buy them in a shop, pick up armfuls of them or take them to your bank. They exist only as concepts and ideas, and even that is stretching the point. Success and failure are just opinions and nothing more.

Everything that you say, think or do produces an outcome or result. If that result is equal to, or greater than, what you aimed for and expected then you will label it as a success. If the result is totally different from your expectations it may still be a success but, in your opinion, you will probably tie the 'failure' label on to it.

Perhaps you have heard of Thomas Edison and his quest to create an electric light bulb. None of his experiments produced the result that he sought, but he did not give up and, as we now know, he eventually succeeded. Edison refused to label all these experiments as failures. Instead, he is reported to have announced that he had discovered 7,000 ways not to make a light bulb. This outlook speaks volumes for his positive way of thinking and his persistent pursuit of success.

Before we get to your personal definition, let's consider persistence a little further, along with some different aspects of success.

As a child you learned to crawl, to walk, to talk, to use a toilet, to tell the time, to tie shoelaces, to read and to write. For each of these endeavours you failed more than once. Your parents didn't say, 'Never mind, give up'; instead they encouraged you to keep on keeping on and heaped praise on you when you achieved your objective. By the age of four or five you already had a highly developed sense of success and its associated pleasure or reward, and equally of failure and its sometimes painful or messy consequences. Still, you did not give up. You mastered something and then moved on to acquiring the next level of skill in socially acceptable behaviours.

You repeated similar sequences throughout your education and then into adulthood where, although your criteria may have been more ambitious, you still strived for the pleasure of success and the avoidance of the pain of failure. The difference is that as an adult, you possibly gave up too soon. The only point of hitting your head against a brick wall is that it is a great relief when you stop, so the wisdom of maturity will tell you when it is time to change something.

As I mentioned in my first book, *The Life Coaching Handbook: Everything You Need To Be An Effective Life Coach*, to remain within an imagined prison, to retain beliefs and to repeat behaviours, while expecting a different outcome, can be compared to a trapped wasp. It will continue to fly into the windowpane, time and time again, until it dies. It never looks for alternative escape routes. It just keeps flying at the glass. Performing the same task, in the same way, and expecting different results has been offered as a definition of madness. With total self-honesty, you have probably done just this and you are still getting the same results.

Please note that I said 'change' and not 'quit'. If your actions do not produce the results that you want, then change one thing at a time. If you change too much in one go, you will not know which change worked for you.

An outcome may be construed as a success by one person and a failure by another. That is why it is essential to construct your very own description of personal success. A burglar who robs a stately home, gets away with his haul and then sells it for an ill gotten gain will think he has had a successful mission. The home owner and his or her insurance company will see the event as a failure of their security systems and routines.

I recently saw a young couple leaving a building society. They scarcely looked old enough to be married let alone have a babe in arms and they were bright eyed and excited. It was obvious from their conversation that they had just been approved for their first mortgage on a dream house. To them, it was a success. To my companion, who was old enough to have been around the block several dozen times and who had a somewhat pragmatic view of life, it was failure because, in his words, 'They have just tied a mill-stone of debt around their necks, yet in their innocence they see it as a milestone of achievement.'

That is probably more than enough philosophising and theory for now, so let's get down and dirty with your own definition of personal success.

So what is success to you?

As you work and play your way through this book you will find a regular sprinkling of 'Self Diagnostic Boxes' along with a few charts and tables for you to pause, think and then act by writing in whatever answers seem right to you at the time. Don't ponder too long as the answer that immediately springs to mind is usually the truest.

Here is the first one and I warn you now that although the question is easy, the answer may not be.

SELF DIAGNOSTIC BOX
SELF
DIAGNOSTIC
BOX
How do I define personal success right now?

Write down your answer (preferably in a notebook) in no more than 20 or so words before you carry on reading.

Now check what you have just written and select one of the categories below:

A. Did you write about a success that you have achieved in the past?
B. Did you write about a success that has been achieved by someone else whom you admire?
C. Did you write about some success that you would like to achieve in the future?

If your answer was A, then you have at least taken the first step in identifying what success meant to you once upon a time. As someone famous once said (it may even have been me!): 'Your past does not equal your future.' So, from this point on, promise yourself that your answers will always be in the 'now' or 'future'. Your past is only useful for the experience that you gained and the lessons that you learned.

If your answer was B, then please note and remember that your personal success is about you and not about someone else. Their success, like their opinion, is theirs not yours and, as your parents probably taught you, it is wrong to take what isn't yours. By all means use the examples of your heroes to inspire you and to motivate you towards your own success; however, this handbook is about personal success, and that means YOU!

A 'C' answer is the best, so well done if you chose that one. You can move on to the next part. For A and B categories, start again and this time, write about your future success.

When I have used this exercise in my seminars and training sessions, there is

> # SELF DIAGNOSTIC BOX
>
> **If my answer was A or B, then answer again— how do I define personal success right now?**

often a sticking point because the global concept of future and personal success is something that is new to many. The answer is to chunk it down into smaller components and to focus on each one in turn.

The chapter headings in this handbook will give you some good ideas of areas to consider and you will come up with ideas of your own. These will usually be in the areas of your life where you currently feel a degree of concern, stress or dissatisfaction.

So now, consider as many elements as you can think of. I have added some ideas in the table below to get you started and there are spaces for your own additions. Ready? Go!

List the areas of your life where you seek success:

- Personal relationships
- Work relationships
- Emotional happiness
- Business
- Interviews
- Career/Work
- Entrepreneurial activity
- Finances/Wealth
- Qualifications
- Sales/Marketing/Influencing
- Spiritual
- Goals
- Health
- Leadership

Select your top three elements from the above list, then identify *just one* of them as your prime success goal right now. You can change your mind later and flip back and forth but, for now, please focus your thoughts on just that one.

Collecting your ingredients

Moving on, you are invited to think of your personal success as a recipe made up of various ingredients in specific measures or volumes. You have selected just one of the areas of your life from the last activity and now I want you to select the most important ingredients for success in that area.

Here is another list for you; which of these 31 keywords do you believe is most directly related to your ability to achieve that success? I have presented them alphabetically, but I want you to mark them in your personal order, with 1 being the most important to you achieving success in that area of your life and 31 the least important.

Alphabetic order	Your order
Academic qualifications	
Age	
Assets	
Chance	
Creativity	
Determination/Drive	
Economic background	
Emotional intelligence	
Enthusiasm	
Entrepreneurial skills	
Ethnicity	
Experience	
Financial skills	
Gender	
Influencing skills	
Intelligence	
Interpersonal skills	
Leadership	
Location	
Luck	
Motivation	
Networking	
Opportunity	

Alphabetic order	Your order
Passion	
Persistence	
Personality	
Physical attributes	
Self-confidence	
Spirituality	
Status	
Talents	

If you placed Passion, Determination and Motivation somewhere in your top five, then as long as the other two were not Luck or Chance, you are well on your route to personal success.

We'll consider the power of those top three attributes shortly, but first, a few lines on the possible relevance of each of the others in your success quest. You might have identified other keywords as you worked down the list; if so, put them in your list and mark them.

Academic qualifications

Academic qualifications are essential for some vocations, professions and careers. To study for examinations and pass them satisfactorily is indeed a success but for most of you it will be a past success that we discussed earlier in this chapter. There are countless examples of people who achieved outstanding success in their chosen fields and who had no academic qualifications and only the most basic education. Their lack can be a red herring of an excuse. If you have qualifications, then that's great. If you don't, then unless you are 100 per cent certain that they are essential for your future success, to chase them for their own sake is at best a waste of time and, at worst, an ego trip. Academia for its own sake is not an ingredient that you need to succeed, so use it as a hobby. Embarking on a study course rather than contributing directly to your success can distract your focus from your main outcome.

Age

Age is immaterial. Some entrepreneurs achieve great success in their teens or early twenties. Other successes come much later in life, even at retirement age and beyond. Discount your age as an ingredient and never, ever use it as an excuse.

Assets

Assets can be as much of a hindrance as a help. If you start with nothing you have nowhere to go but up and your success potential will not be hampered by any doubts or fears that you might lose everything. If you have assets, then do as much as you can to ring-fence them and never 'bet the farm', but use them wisely.

Chance

Chance is an absolute non-starter. If you trust to chance, then you will fail. Chance is essentially placing your fate in the lap of the gods. All successful people take control of their own destiny by taking positive actions that leave nothing to chance and they create their own results.

Creativity

Creativity can be the fundamental ingredient of success or a small factor depending on what you want to achieve. Finding creative solutions to accomplishing your goals could be the difference between success and failure.

Drive

Drive is a close relative of determination. A word of caution is needed here. Most of us have, at sometime or other, missed the slip road off a motorway and had to drive many miles to get back on course. You could drive all day, week, month or year but, unless you are heading in the right direction, you will never reach that destination marked success. Drive with care.

Economic background

Economic background is another excuse rather than being an ingredient. I am sure you can think of successful individuals in almost every sphere of human activity who came from impoverished or humble backgrounds. Some claim that it was a determination never to return to those beginnings that fuelled their success.

Emotional intelligence

Emotional intelligence is based on your ability to observe emotions and feelings whilst being able to differentiate them when considering your own and other people's ways of thinking and behaving to achieve your desired outcomes in a congenial manner.

Enthusiasm

Enthusiasm should be in your top five. It is as contagious as a smile and will encourage people to help you when you need it. It is what will keep you going when the going gets tough.

Entrepreneurial skills

If you know or suspect that you have an entrepreneurial flair, you will probably find your success by doing your own thing. If you lack these skills and the motivation to learn them, your path should follow a more structured career progression.

Ethnicity

Ethnicity is immaterial. Every race, creed and colour has its examples of successful people. It is true that some ethnic backgrounds will find it more difficult than others to succeed in certain locations in the world, but think of the diversity of cultures in Britain's annual 'Rich List' published by the *Sunday Times*. Of course, this list only measures success in financial terms but all ethnicities are represented in most other lists of successful people too.

Experience

Experience is a difficult one to qualify because, although it is obviously based in your past, it may have an impact on your future success. Bad experience should be left behind as long as you learned the lessons that it taught. Good experience can be useful as long as it has breadth and depth. Too many people claim great experience when all they have in reality is small experience constantly repeated. Experience may be useful; it is not essential.

Financial skills

Financial skills will be important when you are considering goals which require some funding or financial management to be successful or for wealth generation, and to ensure that you maintain the discipline of financial control.

Gender

Gender may have been an impediment to success in the past. It is now a neutral ingredient for success, as people of both sexes find success every day.

Influencing skills

Influencing skills can give you the outcomes you are looking for by influencing others to your way of thinking and, coupled with enthusiasm, passion or motivation, can be a very powerful mix.

Intelligence

Intelligence is relative and another neutral ingredient. You can achieve some success without it, as many television reality shows have demonstrated. You can also achieve success with it.

Interpersonal skills

Interpersonal skills will be important where interaction with other people is important to your goal achievement and can be a means towards the end result, but are often not the most important factor.

Leadership

Leadership skills will be important if you are working on a goal which requires these specific skills and can be very important for promotion into managerial roles.

Location

Location can be changed. Depending on the fields of your planned success it may be important. However, you should not allow where you live to be an excuse for lack of success. Successful people never make excuses. They take action instead.

Luck

Yes, the more you act the luckier you will become but, for the purposes of this book, consider luck in the same category as every other fairy story you were told as a child. Successful people create their own luck.

Networking

Networking is another way of suggesting that 'who you know is more important than what you know'. It is obvious that the more people you know, the more nuances of opinion, attitude and talent you will be exposed to, so that you can learn from them. Beware of fair weather friends and those who would seek to rain on your parade. Your network is only as strong as its weakest link.

Opportunity

Opportunity comes into the same category as chance and luck. Your success skill comes in recognising the potential in any opportunity, in assessing its true value and then taking appropriate action. Successful people do not wait for opportunity to knock at their door. They go out and make their own opportunities.

Persistence

Persistence is a useful quality as long as you know when to change direction to achieve the results that you desire.

Personality

Personality is something that everyone has. It can be developed to enhance your expectation of success but there are as many successful people with truly odious personalities as there are with delightful personalities.

Physical attributes

Physical attributes are important as they may limit the areas where you seek success. You truly can be, do or have whatever you want as long as your goals are within your physical abilities. If you have a fear of flying you would not find success as a pilot until you addressed your phobia. If you are short, obese and elderly you will find it almost impossible to achieve success as a sprint athlete.

Know your physical limitations and consider ways to develop them if they are at odds with your desires.

Self-confidence

Self-confidence matters only if you lack it. People who have self-confidence do not consider it to be important because they have it and that is as it should be. If you are lacking in self-confidence you will need to pay attention to addressing this as it could reduce your success rates.

Spirituality

Spiritual consciousness will be important if you are seeking spiritual growth and/or are impacted by people who are spiritually aware and it is a requirement to interact with them.

Status

Status only matters to shallow people who measure success against false yardsticks. A low financial or social status can be a great spur to move you towards success but, in every case and without exception, you can only begin to build success from where you are now.

Talents

Talents are natural gifts. Know what yours are and develop them constantly. Look beyond the obvious for talents that you may have yet to discover. They are useful ingredients but they are not essential for success.

Which leaves us with the top three attributes: *Passion, Determination* and *Motivation*.

Passion, determination and motivation are inseparable and essential ingredients in your recipe for success. They are the fuel that

15

will power your journey; that will keep you going when you hit a snag. They will enable you to turn stumbling blocks into stepping stones.

Passion, determination and motivation are what get you out of bed in the morning, keen to get on with the day ahead. They give you the certain knowledge that you will cope with whatever the day may bring. If you do not like what it delivers, it is within your power to change your attitude and thus your feelings.

With these three attributes alone, you will succeed even if you lack all the other ingredients. Without them, you will fail. It is as simple as that!

Bearing in mind all that you have read so far—for the third time of asking—how do you define your personal success right now?

Having established these ground rule aspects of your definition, in the rest of this handbook we will look at specific areas of success. But first, all successful people honour their promises and earlier I promised you my generic definition of success.

Personal success is when your thoughts, words and actions deliver the results or outcomes that you desire and expect.

SELF DIAGNOSTIC BOX

How do I define my personal success right now?

Success Box

1. Create your own definition of success

2. Identify a prime area of your life

3. Work on your passion

4. Develop determination

5. Sustain your motivation

Action I Will Take

Completed on:

/   /

Action I Will Take

Completed on:

/   /

Action I Will Take

Completed on:

/   /

Action I Will Take

Completed on:

/   /

Action I Will Take

Completed on:

/   /

Action I Will Take

Completed on:

/   /

Chapter Two

Goal Success

If you do not know where you are going, you cannot plan a journey or know when you get there.

This is true for your life journey as well.

Synopsis

This chapter reveals the 'secrets' of successful goal setting and achievement as it spells out exactly what you must do to achieve every goal that you set for yourself on your life purpose—with purpose.

Like the rest of his school pals, Patrick Ian Calhoun would pass his most boring lessons by doodling with his initials. Very soon every book cover, ruler, school bag and anything else that he owned was emblazoned with a stylistic 'PIC'. Unsurprisingly, he was soon known by everyone as Pic which he agreed was a welcome change from Paddy, a name which had plagued him until then and was not really appropriate for someone of his ethnic background.

Although he was not a spoilt child, he received the camera that he coveted for his thirteenth birthday. At Christmas, he was given a box of gadgetry so that he could temporarily convert the family bathroom into a darkroom where he taught himself the arcane art of film processing. The years passed slowly until it was time to leave school and Pic's father and the careers master both told him that there was no security in photography, so he had 'better shape up and seek a proper job'. Pic was accepted as a trainee in the marketing office of a local furniture factory.

He still followed photography as a serious hobby and covered his costs by taking pictures of the firm's outings and various sports and social events, which he sold to his co-workers. His enthusiasm and talent allowed him to create some spectacular shots which came to the notice of the marketing manager who offered Pic an assignment to photograph the forthcoming range for a new catalogue. Pic's reward was an invitation to the annual Florida motivational seminar that the company had arranged to keep the sales team focused. The speaker who discussed goal setting made a particular impact on him and it was one that was to transform Pic's life over the next three years.

As a direct result of following the speaker's instructions and setting goals, he was soon covering local weddings and then, from conversations with seasoned professionals, he discovered that serious money could be made at the high society end of the market. He set a new goal that he would be the best in the area, which would also mean that he could charge top rates.

Pic offered a silent prayer of thanks to that seminar speaker every time he went to the bank. He was solidly booked for big weddings each weekend of the year and then shared any extra bookings out to two trusted associates that he had trained in his style. They would pay him half the fees they earned. His standard fee now starts at £4,000 a booking, which means that he grosses at least £8,000 every weekend. Pic has four days a week free to enjoy his luxury beach front home and sports car. In just four weekends he earns more than his father or careers master could earn in a year. He wonders what the motivational speaker is earning but, alas, he cannot recall the man's name.

Pic, in addition to the wedding shoots, now runs marketing seminars for struggling professional photographers and always makes a point of telling them that the key to his success was learning to set goals and then to take action to achieve them. He tells them never to believe that there is no security in their chosen job because you create your own security by being the best.

This will sound familiar to you. You have a thought that becomes a wish. Then the wish becomes a dream. However, because you know that dreams are the stuff of fantasy, you forget it and get on with your life. Only every once in a while, you will have a dream that is so powerful that you cannot forget it. It can become a nagging desire. More than that, it can become an obsession.

Walt Disney conceived and perpetuated the idea that 'when you wish upon a star, your dreams may come true'. His dream of setting up an amusement park where you charged people to enter became a reality because of his beliefs and commitment to continue to take action regardless of setbacks. So what will you do with your thoughts and wishes? You can dismiss them forever, or you can act upon them. So consider this easy formula:

WISH + DESIRE = GOAL

GOAL + ACTION = FULFILMENT

That is what goal success is all about. If it is that easy, then surely everyone would do it and enjoy a successful life of happy fulfilment? Well, it is that easy and I am about to give you the tools that will allow you to set and achieve your goals. Not for everyone, just for you, and that is the first vital point that you must engrave indelibly on your mind—you can only set goals for yourself and never attempt to do so for other people. Goal setting and achievement demand a degree of selfishness.

The opposite of selfishness is selflessness and you can have that too when your goals bring you such success that you have quality time and valuable assets to share with your nearest, your dearest, and with as many others as you decide to include. Are you ready to be selfish for a few minutes each day when you know that the end result will justify the means? Before you answer that question, consider what a 'no' answer means.

'No' means that you are totally content to drift through life with little or no sense of purpose. 'No' means that whatever will be, will be. 'No' means that you relinquish control of your life to others who may be total strangers. 'No' means that you may never achieve what you desire or deserve in life. 'No' means that you will have an existence but you will not have a full spectrum life. 'No' also means that you are totally satisfied with every aspect of your life and have achieved perfection, which is highly improbable and may require a quick but thorough examination of your conscience.

On the other hand, 'Yes' means that you will be in full control of your own destiny, that you accept full responsibility for everything that happens to you and that you will enjoy success as you move ever closer to everything that you sincerely desire to be, do or have.

'YES', shouted loud and clear with passion is the only acceptable answer!

It is obviously true that people have achieved success, and will continue to do so, without any awareness of goal setting. Their instincts and intuition drive them forward to achieve whatever they set their minds to. I believe that, by using the information contained in this chapter, they would have gained those outcomes even faster and with fewer mistakes along the way. You can achieve your goals with enjoyable ease. First, you must create space.

Put the garbage out

To set and achieve your goals you must make room for them in your life. This means that you must put the garbage out. In these days of recycling and awareness of 'green' issues, you will be familiar with the inducements to sort your garbage. So let's get sorting.

The biggest garbage bin is for limiting excuses. The list which follows on the opposite page includes the most feeble excuses that you can conceive and yet, you may currently use any or all of them every day to limit your freedoms and your opportunities for action. Understand this; these are excuses, they are not reasons. They will keep you in your cosy comfort zone where you will never find and pursue your true destiny.

They are all pretty ridiculous aren't they? Even so, every life coach has heard them regularly and with sadness because the client so often believes that they are true. A good rule often taught during childhood is that we should always keep our promises. I want you to make some powerful promises to improve your own life and then abide by the rules and keep promises that you make to yourself. Please make that resolve right now. Promise yourself that you will never, ever, use or repeat any of these excuses or any other excuses which prevent you from achieving your life goals.

I am	I am
Too old	In the wrong place
Too young	In the wrong time
Too fat	In the wrong house
Too thin	In the wrong job
Too tall	In the wrong clothes
Too short	In the wrong anything!
Too stupid	My boss wouldn't like it
Too intelligent	My spouse wouldn't like it
Too beautiful	My mum wouldn't like it
Too ugly	My cat or dog wouldn't like it
Too lazy	My _____ wouldn't like it!
Too busy	I cannot do it
Too rich	I am afraid of it
Too poor	I am afraid of the dark
Too anything!	I believe in the bogeyman

Your next garbage bin is for your previous failures and experiences. They may have served you well in the past and they may be part of your behaviour patterns, however when it comes to your new goals, there is no room for them or their influences. Goal success is about the now, and about your brilliant future. The past does not, cannot and will not equal the future if you decide not to let it. Using the process of setting goals and taking actions to achieve them means your future will not equal your past; it will be what you choose to allow it to be. Make better choices!

Depending on where you are, who you are and your ethnic background, you may find this next tip difficult, kinky or ludicrous. It is none of these and you need only do it once. When you are home alone and will not be disturbed, find the biggest mirror in your house. Strip off all your clothes, including jewellery, and stand in front of that mirror for one minute. What you see is what you have got to work with, as naked as the day that you were born. Observe yourself from every angle. Be neither critical nor judgemental and then get dressed. If you are ever tempted to consider your goals in the light of what has gone before, just recall this unusual activity and even allow yourself a smile. Within the context of your goals you are a blank canvas. Your life is naked from now on, so that you can build upon it and dress it in any way that you like. Yes! YOU!

Assuming that you have now put your clothes on, it is time to go shopping for a notebook and pen that you will use for your goal purposes and nothing else. You will keep this in a private and secure place and you will discover why I have asked you to do this later in the chapter.

I always recommend that you keep your goals to yourself until you have achieved them. It is far more satisfying to say, 'I have achieved it' than to say, 'I am going to do it'. Let others marvel at your success and wonder how you did it. The only exception to this guidance is when you need to involve someone else to help you towards your objective. If you go public in advance or too soon, there is a risk that others will feel threatened by your deter-mination, that your plans might conflict with their own personal agendas and that they might sabotage your best efforts through their negative emotions of envy or fear.

Unless your goal is written down, it has little chance of being real-ised. There is an amazing synergy that occurs between mind and body from the sheer act of writing. When you write you will also be communicating with your incredibly powerful subconscious mind that always strives to deliver whatever you ask of it, with-out question. Apart from any psychological phenomenon, there is always the possibility that you will forget your goal unless you write it down. As you might expect by now, there is a correct way to write goals to enhance their achievement.

Another reason for committing your goal to paper is that you must read it aloud, at least twice a day. The best times for this are first thing in the morning and last thing at night. I have just mentioned that your subconscious mind is incredibly powerful. It is, but it also has a childlike simplicity where constant repetition brings rapid results, and it is most receptive when you are in those twilight states immediately before and after sleep.

There are two more vital ingredients in your recipe for goal success. One of them is about timing and the other is about how you write your goals. We shall return to both after this brief summary of the story so far:

1. Dispose of your garbage
2. Forget the past
3. Goals are now and future
4. Do the naked mirror minute
5. Acquire a notebook
6. Be secretive
7. Write your goals
8. Repeat them twice daily

SELF DIAGNOSTIC BOX

Have I decided to get a notebook? When will I do so?

All goals are not equal

Goals come in diverse shapes and sizes, a point worth remembering when you are defining your goals. If I asked a group of delegates to write down their goals, a few might scribble something but most of them would gaze at me with a look of perplexed bewilderment.

Because the scope of individual goals is so massive, you need a method of sorting them out. To prepare for this, take your notebook and across the top of a blank page, write GOAL CATEGORY: Family. On the next page, write Work and then continue to head up pages for as many areas of your life as you can think of. Other categories might be Sport, Career, Finance, Relationships, Home, Cars, Hobbies and so on.

The next step is to take each of these pages at a time and to divide them roughly into three columns. Head the first column as Short, the middle one as Medium and the last one as Long. As you consider each page and timeframe, jot down key words about your wishes in the appropriate columns. Please note that these are only reminders of things that you would like and they are not yet goals. You will find an example below.

Short-term items should be those that could be done, fixed or achieved within the next few days or weeks if you set your mind to them. Let's say they can be done in less than a month from now. Medium term covers those that would take up to a year and long term covers a period of more than a year.

As you write, avoid any form of censorship as anything goes regardless of whether you can afford the time or money to make them happen. Leave the how, or any other limitations, at the moment and just let your mind roam free, writing the ideas as they pop into your mind. Above all, have fun.

You will certainly think of other things as time goes by so return to your lists as often as you need to and write down these ideas as they occur to you. There are no right or wrong answers!

GOAL CATEGORY: *Home*

Short	Medium	Long
Clean kitchen	*Redecorate bedroom*	*Paint exterior of house*
Fix broken cupboard	*Buy plasma television*	*Put house on market*
Steam clean carpets	*Have drive resurfaced*	*Move to Devon*
Weed the garden	*Get trees pruned*	

Your juicy goal

Ask a hundred people what they want in life above everything else, and most people will give you a list of things that they don't want! That at least is a starting point because each of these negatives can be turned into its positive equivalent. For example, 'I don't want

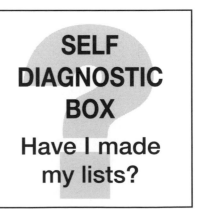

SELF DIAGNOSTIC BOX
Have I made my lists?

to work in an office' could become 'I do want to work outdoors in the open air'.

We can return to the fun aspects of goal setting in a little while. First, I invite you to give some serious thought to the next question. It may take you a while to come up with your answer and that is fine as it is vitally important that you do answer.

IF I COULD BE, DO OR HAVE ANYTHING IN MY LIFE, WITH NO RISK OF FAILURE, NO LIMITS AND NO RESPONSIBILITY FOR THE OUTCOMES—WHAT WOULD IT BE?

Please read that question again slowly and carefully because every word is important. Beware of negative thoughts creeping in as you consider your answer. This is a question with no restrictions where anything can be possible.

Take your notebook and write 'My Juicy Goal' at the top of the page and start writing your answer.

When goals collide

It is absolutely fine to have ambitious goals; indeed there can be a tendency to set goals too low. But there is another aspect to the art of goal writing that you need to understand.

Every goal, whether short, medium or long term *must* have a target completion date. To put it another way, a goal without a completion date is just a dream and it seriously reduces the chances of it becoming a reality.

There are three reasons for attaching completion dates to goals.

The first is that it allows you to avoid a situation where goals collide. It would be great to decide to be a doctor and a lawyer. Say each profession has a five year residential study period, then obviously you could do them one after the other, but you could not do them both at the same time.

The second reason for setting completion dates is that they offer a reality check (which is not the same as an excuse!). If your goal is to landscape your garden and you write this goal in December, for example, then it is fine to have a short term goal of detailed planning within the next two weeks. This is not the right time of year for a major planting programme so the timing schedule must include the laws of nature and horticulture to ensure success. All your goal dates need to take into account any natural or prescribed time constraints.

SELF DIAGNOSTIC BOX

Have I checked for goal collisions?

I have kept the most important reason until last. It has been demonstrated and proven that having a target completion date sends a powerful message to your subconscious that will then do all that it can to deliver. It will guide your actions and decision making towards fulfilment. Everything that you say, think or do will bring you closer to your deadlined goal. Without a date your actions may even lead you further away from your goal.

You also need to make brief notes about how you will know when you have achieved your goal. As you read these words you may be thinking, 'Of course I will know', but with the passage of time your focus will not be as sharp as it is right now. A short term goal like fixing a squeaky door is obviously achieved when the door stops squeaking. Goals related to success and earnings need to have this 'how I will know' factor.

So already you have some rules to remember. Your goals must be:

1. Categorised according to specific areas of your life
2. Defined as short, medium and long term
3. Be written with a target completion date and destination reminder
4. Read twice daily

Keeping it positive, present and prioritised

There is another aspect to goal writing that is equally important. Your goals must be written in the present tense, as if they are already a reality. If your short term goal is to clean the kitchen and it is now the morning of Friday February 1, then the way to write this goal is:

It is the afternoon of Saturday February 2 and the kitchen is sparkling after its deep clean and I feel content and pleased with a job well done.

You can follow this procedure for every other goal in your note-book, so return to those earlier pages and, using one new page for every goal, write them out in the present tense with completion dates and how you will feel at having achieved them.

You will probably need to 'chunk down' your goals into smaller ones. Take, for example, the simple aim of buying a plasma television. Your 'chunking down' may suggest the following smaller goals:

• Decide where the television will be located
• Check there are adequate power points
• Check for aerial or dish connections
• Research the brands, size, models and retailers who offer the best price and delivery
• Choose the brand, size, model and retailer who offers the best price and delivery
• Ensure you have the finances arranged to pay for this
• Place the order
• Take delivery and install the television
• Set up payment methods for satellite or cable services

For each stage, write in the present tense and add a completion date.

• It is __/__/__(date) I have decided where the television will be located
• It is __/__/__(date) There are adequate power points

- It is __/___/___(date) I have the aerial/dish connections ready
- It is __/___/___(date) I have researched the brands, size, models and retailers
- It is __/___/___(date) I have chosen the brand, size, model and retailer who offers the best price and delivery and I feel excited about my achievements
- It is __/___/___(date) I have the finances arranged to pay for this
- It is __/___/___(date) I have placed the order
- It is __/___/___(date) The delivery and installation of the television have taken place and I am sitting watching my favourite programme and feeling happy
- It is __/___/___(date) I have set up payment methods for satellite or cable services

When you have completed this phase, which is easier to do than it is to describe, you need to go back to your individual goals pages and prioritise them all in order of their importance to you. Use a coloured pen and mark each goal from 1 to 100 (or whatever) to define the order in which you will achieve them.

Gather your resources

Consider any new skills, qualities, knowledge or equipment that you will need to make each goal happen and follow the rules as you write more goals for acquiring them.

Consider any other people who you will need to involve, such as teachers, partners, spouse, employer, retailer and then, do whatever is needed to bring them on side to share your vision. Communicate clearly and concisely what you are aiming to achieve and their specific role in your achievement.

Take your top prioritised goal in each area of your life and summarise it on a postcard, using one card for each goal. Place these cards in your wallet, bag, car or desk where you can easily find them every day or create files on your computer with daily reminders set to alert you. As I have previously said, read each one twice a day. This regular review is a crucial step to achieving your goals.

It is especially important to read your Juicy Goal every time. Imagine the big picture. See that exam success certificate in your hand, visualise the bank statement with your desired wealth in the credit column, feel the joy of having your soul mate and partner by your side.

In addition to completing the above steps, you may also want to acquire one of the many excellent books that deal exclusively with goal setting and achievement then follow its suggestions. If you cannot find one in your local shop or library, then access the free information on the Internet.

If you have followed these guidelines you will achieve your goals. Your circumstances and situation will change with time and so will your goals. They are words on paper, not set in concrete, so be prepared to change them when you need to.

When you think of acquiring your goal as a journey you will realise that any journey requires energy or fuel. With goals, your fuel is motivation and passion. You will be motivated to move away from discomfort, pain or any situation that is unacceptable to you and this may be what leads you to consider setting a goal in the first instance. When you hold a firm mental picture of a satisfactory outcome, you will be motivated to move towards it. Beware the gap where the pain diminishes but the pleasure has not yet been achieved, for this is the black hole where many goals can slip into oblivion. You have been warned!

Work–life balance

Now you have decided your outcomes and the timeframes within which you will achieve them you need to do a work–life balance check. This means that you plan for successes in all areas of your life including a balance of work, with life outside of work. Notice I did not say 'all areas of your life including a balance of work and pleasure'; this is because I believe if you are successful you will enjoy the work you do along with the time you spend outside of work.

Look at your goal timeframes making sure that you have balanced time between your work goals and allowed time for relaxation, exercise, family, friends, spiritual pursuits, holidays, mini-breaks, hobbies, sports, etc. This means that you balance your time between work and outside of work. It is often perceived that people spend too much time at work but it is also true that many people spend a lot of time watching television (around 37 days per year, according to national statistics) or internet surfing (41 days per year). Now, if you are consciously watching television or surfing the internet as part of your relaxation and recuperation, that is great, only if you are simply channel or site hopping because you cannot be bothered to move, you know you have spare time capacity. If this is you, think what you could achieve with this time if you used it working towards your success goals. What could you achieve if you used just 50 per cent of this time, 18-and-half days, or put another way, 444 hours? Think about this—even if you only use half of this television-watching time, you could spend one hour and 13 minutes per day (365 days of the year) on your life purpose or your success goals! With a very simple change in your habits you can achieve wonderful exciting goals so, when would be a great time to make this little change?

Time management

You have decided you are not going to settle for less than the best you can be and now you need to examine how you can achieve being the best. You will need to change your habits and reclaim your time and, as mentioned in the paragraph above, you can do this with a simple change. If you know you waste time watching television simply decide which television programmes you are going to dump, and dump them.

If Internet surfing is your weakness, here is a quick fix, which I have successfully used with many of my

SELF DIAGNOSTIC BOX

How do I spend my non-working time?

clients—buy a free-standing alarm clock (the computer alarm does not produce such good results) and decide exactly how much time you are going to spend surfing. Set your alarm clock. When it rings, STOP SURFING. Now, close the search engine and *move away* from your computer. Moving away from the computer (even if your goals require using the computer) is an essential part of the process as it breaks the surfing mindset and gives you time to refocus. You do not need to be away from the computer for long—a couple of minutes should be sufficient to change your mindset—and when you return to the computer the surfing screen has been closed preventing instant surfing access.

We waste time in so many different ways that it is impossible to cover them all here. I will give you some ideas below and then it is up to you to recognise where you waste time and decide to do something about it. Ask yourself this question: 'When is the first time I look at my emails?' If the answer is as soon as you arrive at the office, ask: 'Do I control this time or do I find that I have spent much longer than I wanted to answering email?' Most people start the day without timeframes or clear outcomes and let their inbox and emails control their days. Use a time blocking system. Decide your outcomes for the day (using a simple to-do list) and block time for all the tasks including time for responding to emails.

Some ideas on how time is wasted	What can be done to change this
Watching TV, surfing the net, computer games, sending texts and chatting on phone, window shopping etc.	Make a record of where you spend your time at the moment. Decide what can be dumped
Treating small problems the same as a full crisis	Before taking action, ask yourself: 'What would happen if I did nothing?'
Inability to say 'no'	You have a choice. Start saying 'no' to small issues—for practise

Some ideas on how time is wasted	What can be done to change this
People assume you will say 'yes'	Decide to change this assumption and practise saying 'no'
You have no strategy for saying 'no'	Say 'no' and follow it with alternative actions for the requester
Wanting to help others regardless of self	Be very clear on your own outcomes/goals. Ask yourself: 'Will doing this take me nearer to my goals or steal time from my achievements?'
Wanting to feel important or needed	Ask yourself: 'Am I doing this just to feel important or needed?' Be honest with yourself
Concern of being disliked for saying 'no'	Think of someone you like who says 'no' and model them
Ambition/desire to be seen to be busy	You will be truly busy if you have clear goals
No time deadlines set when working on tasks	Start setting deadlines. Ask yourself: 'How long will this take?' and use an alarm clock to keep you to that timeframe
Lack of deadlines	Give yourself deadlines and stick to them
No respect for your own valuable time	Be very clear on your own outcomes/goals. Ask yourself: 'Will this take me nearer to my goals?'
Overworked	Before each task consider if there is anyone else who is able do this. Is doing all this going to take you closer to your own outcomes?

Some ideas on how time is wasted	What can be done to change this
Unorganised work loads	Organise yourself and stick to your plans
Not very inspired by certain jobs	Remind yourself of your long term goals to keep you inspired and motivated
Lost your inspiration/ motivation	Remind yourself of your reason for doing the job and how it will take you nearer to your long term goals
Postponing unpleasant tasks	Remind yourself of your long term goals for inspiration and just DO IT!
Responding to the urgent not the important	Be very clear on your own outcomes/goals. Ask yourself: 'Will this take me nearer to my goals?'
Carelessness on rushed jobs	Ask yourself: 'If I have to do this again, what are the costs involved?'
Always work late	Leave on time—or decide exactly how much unpaid time you are willing to work and then leave immediately the time is up. If you have clear personal goals it will be easier to do this
Wanting to be involved in everything by doing the minor things	Ask for end of day reviews and let go! Avoid doing the minor things at the expense of the major things
Unrealistic length of telephone calls—too long on the phone	Decide on your outcome for the call at the beginning and as soon as you have reached it close the call politely

Some ideas on how time is wasted	What can be done to change this
Telephone calls become too involved in details	Ask the other person to send you an email—this allows you to select the time to look at the details
Idle chatting with colleagues	Be polite and brief—it is your life you are impacting by idle chatting
Uncontrolled conversations	Control them now!
Continue working on company stuff during your own lunch break	Stop doing this! Take a full lunch break and use the time on RAWPOWER towards achieving your goals
Too much time spent on telephone calls or emails	Use a time blocking technique. Decide on the times you will handle calls and emails and stick to it

Now put your own personal time wasters in the left column and decide what you are going to do instead in the right column.

How I waste time	What I am going to do about it

Once you have clear compelling outcomes for your life and a 'Juicy Goal' you know what is important and it is easier to decide what to do, and what not to do.

A great question to ask yourself before you take on any tasks or do any activity is: 'Will doing this take me closer to my goals or closer to someone else's goals?'

So, for example, when you are watching television you are working on someone else's goals. Unless you have made the conscious decision to watch the television for a specific time and for a specific reason, you *could* be working on your goals. Now if you are making excuses in your head for wasting time watching television and not concentrating your energies on achieving your own designed destiny, be absolutely aware that you are doing this. Be honest with yourself, excuses are just that! We all have the same amount of time in a day, a week, a month or a year—it's how we use this time that makes the difference between attaining successful outcomes and just drifting along.

Walking my talk

I have followed every tip in this chapter to create this book. Initially I had little notion of how I could write another book in my already busy schedule but, with the experience of two other books behind me, I was able to set really accurate goals with target dates, and I put aside time each day to work on this goal. I also celebrated the completion of each chapter and subsequent editing stage by rewarding myself with a small treat. And then I planned a big treat for publication day. Give yourself treats in proportion to the measures of your achievements.

Goal setting with step-by-step plans of action to achieve the goals should be fun. If you feel excited as you contemplate your goals you are on the path to success in your life journey and to reaching the destination you want to arrive at.

Action Box

1. Write your rough lists of wishes

2. Write them as instructed above to turn them into goals

3. Read them twice daily

4. Take action to bring them nearer every day

5. Identify how you waste time, and make changes

6. Celebrate your achievements

Action I Will Take

Completed on:

/   /

Action I Will Take

Completed on:

/   /

Action I Will Take

Completed on:

/   /

Action I Will Take

Completed on:

/   /

Action I Will Take

Completed on:

/   /

Action I Will Take

Completed on:

/   /

Chapter Three

Health Success

Good health or bad health—each has an impact on your success.

Synopsis

This chapter looks at the components of health and how to maintain a healthy body—and it comes with a health warning!

John Bond had just completed the introduction section of the sales presentation he was delivering when the pain struck. He felt a relaxation in his face, followed by limpness in his right arm. He started to panic and asked the delegates for help but as he started to speak the words became slurred and incomprehensible. A delegate rushed forward whilst another dialled her mobile for medical help. All the time the symptoms were getting worse. Someone was speaking to him but he could not see clearly. He blinked his eyes to clear his vision but it did not help and his vision was becoming blurred like his speech.

The next thing John remembered was hearing his wife's voice calling his name. He opened his eyes to discover he was in hospital and had had a stroke. Luckily for John, the delegate who dialled for medical assistance had seen the symptoms before so she knew that he was having a stroke and needed to get to hospital as soon as possible.

John made a full recovery but it could have been much worse.

Each year in the United Kingdom, about 110,000 people have their first stroke, and between 28,000 and 30,000 of these have another stroke. Heart failure on the other hand affects around 900,000 people in the UK. One in three people will be diagnosed with cancer in the UK (like myself, in 1992). There are many elements that have been attributed to causing illness and disease, including diet, lifestyle, environment, mental attitude, stress levels and so on. There are also several factors which contribute to the general meaning and feeling of good health, and these would normally include good mental health. In this chapter, we are going to focus on the physical side of good health to encourage you to respect and nurture your body. The reason this topic is covered so early in the book is because I have found that when our bodies are not capable of functioning or performing well, and when our energy levels are depleted, a negative effect occurs which impacts all the other areas of our lives and reduces our chances of attaining successful outcomes.

What does good health mean to you?

I realise this may seem a strange thing to ask you to consider. The reason I ask is because we are all at different levels of health and for some of us good health would just mean being able to walk up the street without getting out of breath. For others it means being full of energy. You need to determine your own definiton of health before you will know if you have it or not. Spend some time thinking about the answer and write it down in your notebook.

> **SELF DIAGNOSTIC BOX**
>
> In line with my own definition of good health, where am I now?

You are what you eat!

There are many sayings about what we eat such as, 'rubbish in, rubbish out', 'eat fat, grow fat', 'over the lips and on to the hips' and many more. There are hundreds of diet books, good food guides, television programmes, CDs and MP files all dedicated to the food we eat.

Every week there is new research which tells us 'this is bad for you', 'this is good for you' and, yes, you are right, they are talking about the same foods! Most of us are not told where the funding for the research comes from. This is the key to fully understanding research findings. Just imagine for a moment: a vegetarian food manufacturer wants to promote vegetarian food and sponsors research into the bad effects of eating meat compared to eating vegetables. The results of the research will reflect the statement of intent of the original research. This means that because the statement of intent is searching for the bad effects of eating meat, this is where the focus and findings will materialise. It is all about focus. Let me prove this in a simple way so that you understand what I mean.

Activity

Pick a colour, any colour. I am going to use yellow for this activity. Now look around you and find everything that is yellow. Look behind, to your sides, above and below. Go on! Have a good look.

Now, answer this question: 'How many blue things did you see?' 'That's not fair,' I hear you say! 'You told me to look for yellow things.' Yes, I did and that is what often happens with research. The outcome (looking for yellow) is stated before the research has begun, therefore the researchers are researching within previously defined parameters and will usually find what they are looking for. Add to this the fact that research has to be funded, so the research will probably report findings in line with or supporting the funding organisation's viewpoint. So, going back to your activity, if you are specific in what you are looking for (yellow or your colour) it is an odds-on favourite that you will always find it.

Taking this in light of all the research that we are bombarded with about foods being good or bad for us, we can now view the research with a more cautious approach by seeking the initial criteria and knowing who funded it.

Now there is another factor involved here, and that is your personal filtering. In the activity above I gave you the opportunity to select your own colour for a reason. As soon as you selected the colour, you have taken a more personal involvement in the activity and will have probably looked a little bit harder to find items displaying the colour you selected. Either way, you will have filtered out most of the other colours in your vicinity to complete the task. This means that when you read the findings of research you will also filter out information you do not want to see and information which does not match your beliefs. For example, say you absolutely adore chocolate. You are more likely to accept research which tells you that chocolate helps you to relax than you are to accept research which states that it has a high fat content which is bad for you. No wonder we are all confused and some of us give up altogether and indulge in our fancies to the detriment of our health.

Eating for success

Try to eat a varied, balanced diet which includes the necessary elements to keep you strong and full of energy, and eat in moderation. If you feel tired and sluggish after a meal, you are not eating for success. You need to feel energised and satisfied after eating and if you do not, review your food intake and make changes. Generally accepted is the rule of eating five portions of a combination of fruit and vegetables per day. A diet low in processed or pre-cooked food is recommended by successful athletes. For those of you who are not sure which foods are

SELF DIAGNOSTIC BOX
What food makes me feel sluggish?

better for you, hire a nutritionalist, do your research and use the RAWPOWER method as described in the Introduction.

Drink

The body is made up of 60 to 80 per cent water depending on what research you look at and the breakdown of that research into bones and blood etc. For our purpose, we only need to be aware that a large part of the body is liquid. Sweating is a natural function, which causes liquid loss. This means we need to drink often throughout the day. Water is being continuously lost and therefore it needs to be replaced in order for us to function. Many people will drink various different types of liquid throughout the day, so providing you drink a fair amount of water every day you can add in a variety of drinks which you enjoy. Particularly good are juices that have been squeezed fresh as you require them because you can select what fruit and vegetables go into the juice and can use high energy or slow releasing energy foods depending on your immediate needs. Remember to avoid or limit your intake of alcohol, caffeine and stimulants with refined sugars added because, although they can give you a quick 'high', there is an energy low that will follow. So keep this in mind and make your decisions based on a long term plan for success rather than a short term fix.

SELF DIAGNOSTIC BOX
How much water do I drink in a day?

An effective way to increase your water intake is to buy a beautiful bottle and a glass. Measure the amount of liquid the bottle holds and fill it with natural mineral water. Put your bottle in a place where you will constantly notice it throughout the day as a reminder to drink more. For example, keep the bottle on your desk if you work in an office. Put your glass next to the bottle and constantly sip water as you work, replenishing the water in the bottle as required. Keep a note of how many times you fill your bottle and you will know how much water you drink during the day.

Exercise

We all know that exercise is good for us so why is it that a large percentage of the population does little or no exercise? I think there are many factors that influence this, such as the power of TV, excessive workloads, stress, time available and our own personal concept of what constitutes exercise.

Several years ago, I was encouraged to do some exercise and was directed towards attending a gym. For many people the gym is a great place to combine exercise, personal hygiene (showering etc.) along with their social life, and that is a great result. For me, however, things were different. I was overweight by four stones and seven pounds in relation to my height. The gym was popular with young women and men wearing designer clothes which fitted their slim bodies perfectly. I am not lacking in self-esteem, yet I often felt conspicuous. Nevertheless, I continued to attend the gym throughout the winter. This particular winter I suffered from an almost continuous cold which occasionally became flu and back to cold again. I was concerned because in previous winters I had suffered only one or two colds. I had many different ideas as to why I was suffering with this prolonged illness, until the day I was in the gym on an exercise bike. I looked up and saw a burly bloke on the running machine. He was coughing, sweating profusely and had a runny nose which he wiped with his hand and placed back on the machine. I watched him go around the gym blowing his nose into his hand or his small towel, which he also used to wipe the machines with. Bingo! I left the gym and have never returned. It was the excuse I needed to free me from the chore of attending a gym. I now know that I am not alone in my dislike of gyms.

I immediately replaced the visits to the gym with jogging. I hated jogging at first and now I love it with a passion. The point I am making is that there is an exercise for everyone and it does not have to be joining a gym. Often when I am coaching a client we will explore all physical activities by making a diverse list, which may include walking, sailing, horse riding, dancing, cycling, swimming, team sports, golf and so

SELF DIAGNOSTIC BOX

What fun activities can I do on a regular basis to increase my physical exercise?

on. The key is for my client to find one or two activities they enjoy, either from the past or that they would love to try, and then to just do it! You will only keep exercising if you enjoy doing it, so select activities you enjoy doing and commit to doing them regularly and have FUN!

If you are short of time and out of shape consider a simple routine change such as walking up a flight of stairs instead of taking the lift on alternate days of the week. A simple change in routine can be the catalyst to you doing more interesting activities and who knows where that will lead.

Laughter

After I was diagnosed with breast cancer and an aggressive form of lymphatic cancer (I was given nine months to live), I devised a series of strategies I now call the RAWPOWER method. Using this method I discovered many interesting and exciting new ideas about health and how to recover it. There are far too many effective ways to improve our health for me to include in this chapter but one discovery which stood out for me is the power of laughter to heal. The fact that laughter heals is based on scientific research (watch out for research as I mentioned before). When we laugh, our bodies pro-duce T-cells, gamma-interferon and B-cells, all of which produce disease and infection-destroying antibodies. Laughter stimulates the release of the body's natural painkillers called endorphins. This all amounts to a general sense of well-being and can speed up recovery. I could not think of a more fun way to aid my recovery and so proceeded to read funny books, watch my favour-ite comedians and attend the theatre to see comedy plays.

> **SELF DIAGNOSTIC BOX**
>
> **When was the last time I had a real belly laugh?**

Rest

It is as important to rest as it is to take exercise to keep yourself healthy. Most people need at least six hours of good revitalising sleep to perform at their peak every day. This is not a rule and you will need to discover your optimum for peak performance. Margaret Thatcher was reported to only need three or four hours of sleep during her years at Downing Street and, regardless of your political persuasion, you must admit she seemed to be working at peak performance levels.

During my recovery I was taking medication that was not helpful to getting a good night's sleep and I learnt during this time that rest does not need to equate to sleep. Rest can be achieved through meditation and relaxation techniques. It can require a change of mindset to allow ourselves to believe that simply resting will give the body time and space to recuperate, for that is the outcome of resting. Most people become agitated when they cannot sleep and start to run negative thoughts and phrases in their minds that keep them awake, such as, 'If I do not get to sleep soon I will not be able to ...' or 'I've been lying here for hours now and I am still not asleep—I will feel dreadful in the morning'. Statements like these only increase your agitation and reduce your chances of getting to sleep. I often use, 'I am resting and recuperating and I feel relaxed. I do not need to be asleep for this to happen.' Knowing that I do not need to sleep to recuperate helps me to sleep!

SELF DIAGNOSTIC BOX

How often do I have time for good quality rest?

Fun and play

I mentioned above that laughter helps recovery and can give a feeling of well-being, and this is also true if you spend time having fun. As adults we often forget to take time for ourselves to just do something for the pure pleasure of doing it, doing it just for fun. This can sometimes be the same activity as you do for exercise which combines the two things within the same timeframe; this is particularly good if you are on a time budget. The sort of things that come to mind are belly dancing, basket ball and ice skating, all of which can be very funny to learn and at the same time allow you to exercise or keep fit.

SELF DIAGNOSTIC BOX

What do I do on a regular basis just for the fun of it?

Activity

List five things you want to do for fun that also have a fitness element.

1. _____

2. _____

3. _____

4. _____

5. _____

Pick one and commit to doing it for one month—and if you can get a friend to join you all the better because you can still laugh about the experience long after it has passed. This will release those good endorphins and strengthen your friendship at the same time.

It is important to keep active no matter what your age or ability. The saying 'Use it or lose it!' comes to mind. It is much healthier to smile than to frown.

Body checks

It is essential to do regular self-checks on your body; if you know how your body feels when you are well, you will be able to feel any changes when they occur. If you are unsure what you need to do then visit your doctor and ask to be shown what you need to do during your self-examination. At the same time, get your doctor to perform a well-man or well-woman check so that you know you are starting from a good health base and then continue to have regular checks by your doctor. If you discover an anomaly you will be able to get help quickly, and early detection usually means you have a far better chance of recovery or survival. Get feeling!

SELF DIAGNOSTIC BOX

When was the last time I attended a well-man or well-woman clinic?

Health covers a multitude of areas all of which have medically qualified experts who have published on their subjects, and I would not presume to usurp them. Therefore, I recommend a RAWPOWER approach to this subject (described in the Introduction) and trust you will find it as fascinating as I did. Once I started seriously studying health I completely changed my diet, introduced regular exercise into my daily routines, started taking vitamin and mineral supplements, having regular massages, meditating, having regular fun and much, much more. This chapter comes with a health warning—once you start on this fascinating journey using the RAWPOWER method when considering your health, your life will never be the same!

Success Box

1. Write a list of fun things to do

2. Learn how to perform a self-check

3. Eat a varied healthy diet

4. Drink plenty of water or fresh juice

5. Do an exercise you enjoy

Action I Will Take

Completed on:

/   /

Action I Will Take

Completed on:

/   /

Action I Will Take

Completed on:

/   /

Action I Will Take

Completed on:

/   /

Action I Will Take

Completed on:

/   /

Action I Will Take

Completed on:

/   /

Chapter Four

Emotional Success

*Unless you control your emotions, your emotions will control you.
There are no other options and you must be in control if you are to
maintain a healthy emotional balance.*

Synopsis

This chapter offers a definition of emotion; it lists the most common ranges of emotions and outlines their corresponding behaviours. You are offered some examples of emotional behaviour so that you can determine which apply to your own circumstances.

Theresa Dalveen grew up in a loving family. She would truthfully claim that in all her life she had never heard her father raise his voice in anger. Even so, she knew when she had misbehaved because, rather than shouting, he would speak even more quietly than usual, carefully enunciating every word in his deep Dublin brogue.

She once, and only once, raised her voice to him over something that had seemed important to her at the time. 'That was your first time, my girl, and while you live in this house it will be the last,' he told her as his bright blue eyes blazed into her own. She knew that she was loved but the pain in his expression and the implied threat in his low voice made her resolve never to hurt him again by further transgressions.

This was just one of many childhood 'rules of the house' that she learned and carried through into adulthood. She sometimes grinned as she took her outdoor shoes off whenever she entered her own house and recalled seeing her brothers' and sisters' shoes or slippers lined up in strict order of size. Another was the habit of always carefully folding or hanging her clothes and putting them away instead of dropping them on the floor. She even counted to ten and took three deep breaths before she criticised or judged another person. 'To be sure, 'tis better to say nothing unless I can say something good,' was another childhood lesson that she had learned well.

Theresa was a passionate woman who felt very strongly about many causes, but it was her calm demeanour, largely nurtured by her parents, that won her promotion to team leader in the air-traffic control centre where she had made her career. At the selection interview she had been told, 'We are offering you this job because, although the other candidates had equal experience and skills, your calm and unemotional outlook tells us that you will cope confidently and well if any emergency arises during your spells on duty.'

Her father had long since passed away, but as she drove home, she often offered him a quiet prayer of thanks for having showed her the importance of emotional balance.

In general, and as in many of the other chapters in this book, success is commonly defined in material terms. This is understandable because these can easily be seen and measured against some specific criteria, typically their financial worth.

When dealing with success at an emotional level, we have no such ready reckoner. There is no rule of thumb, and yet there are as many definitions of emotional success as there are souls on this planet for we each have our own parameters. This means that I can make my own meaning of emotional success without any fear of contradiction.

SELF DIAGNOSTIC BOX

Am I able to control my emotional states?

Therefore, I have identified three parts to the meaning of emotional success:

1. When your negative emotions do not hold you back or restrict your freedom in any way

2. When you are fully in control of your emotions and can easily switch to a positive emotional state when you need to
3. When you express and acknowledge your emotions appropriately according to the circumstances

While we are thinking about definitions, I suppose I should also say what I mean by 'emotional' in this context.

It is obviously to do with emotions, and emotions can be thought of as feelings which may manifest in actions. We are all emotional to a greater or lesser degree. You may wear your heart on your sleeve and allow your actions to reveal your emotions to anyone within sight or earshot, or you may have been taught to retain that mythical 'British stiff upper lip' and keep your emotions securely bottled up and corked. The downside to this latter option is that, like a champagne bottle being shaken, when some event or some innocent bystander triggers a release, the stuff of your emotions just sprays everywhere indiscriminately.

Consider this scenario from my own experience. I was working in a vast open plan office where all the staff worked at their own work stations. One woman received a personal telephone call which the receptionist had put through to her, even though this was against the house rules. She did so because she thought it was important. The woman burst into tears, shouted 'Oh my God!' and ran from the office knocking her phone, coffee cup and computer monitor off her desk as she did so. Her supervisor, alarmed by this conduct, followed her to the restroom where the woman was sobbing her heart out. It transpired that the telephone call was to tell her that an aunt, with whom she had never been particularly close, had died unexpectedly and suddenly. The woman went home and took compassionate leave until after the funeral.

A few months later, another colleague received a similar call. She got up from her desk, had a quiet word with the supervisor and went slowly out of the building where she walked around the car park for ten minutes before returning to her work. She later explained that she needed that short time out to consider all the implications of the news and to prioritise her thoughts concerning any responsibilities that might fall to her as a result.

The first woman displayed overt emotional stress while the second woman, who doubtless felt a similar degree of loss, behaved unemotionally. This does not mean that she was not emotionally affected by the news, just that she handled the information in a more appropriate manner and was able to control her emotional responses to external stimuli.

Neither was totally right nor wrong beyond the obvious point that the first woman had disrupted the office for several minutes and distracted everyone from their tasks. She also ran the risk of earning a reputation which might not serve her promotional prospects in the future. It was the actions triggered by the emotions that differed in each instance.

SELF DIAGNOSTIC BOX

How do I react when given dreadful information while at work?

Of course these are extreme cases that demonstrate the differences. Whether you consider yourself emotional or not, your actions can still be evoked by an emotional response to some outside stimulus, even if it has no personal connection with you. You may have cried during a particularly sad film, you have surely laughed at a great comedy and it is almost certain that you will have bought some snack even though you weren't really hungry until you caught the smell of frying onions from a burger stall at an outdoor event. Emotions then are cognitive processes that create actions by stimulating your senses and can be totally alien to reason or rationality. Let us consider a hit parade of human emotions.

Here we have five main categories of emotions and most secondary examples will fit into one or more of them. They are:

1. Love
2. Happiness
3. Anger

4. Sadness
5. Fear

Hopefully, you will have experienced love, either as a recipient or a donor, or ideally both at the same time. You will certainly have experienced all the others.

Just to get you started on seeing how other emotions fit into these five main categories, here are a few examples not given earlier.

- **Love** can include respect, lust, admiration, worship, desire, excitement
- **Happiness** can include excitement, satisfaction, pride, calmness, confidence
- **Anger** can include jealousy, irritation, hatred, disgust, frustration
- **Sadness** can include disappointment, pity, distress, boredom, depression
- **Fear** can include nervousness, remorse, confusion, hope, carefulness

This hit-parade list is by no means complete but it is enough to start working with the many dimensions of your emotions. It also shows that emotions cover a vast range of which normally you would only feel one emotion at a time. Even so, it is possible for one emotion to trigger another; for example, laughing at a joke—a happiness emotion—can lead to admiration for the joke teller.

It is also possible for emotions to cascade through a range. Take the instance of a personal loss through death or divorce. You may feel an initial emotion of shock followed by disbelief. This may gradually mutate into anger before sadness and disappointment. These may lead to guilt, then blame and ultimately fear. Over a short period you could experience a whole array of emotions. Hopefully, you will rarely experience events that lead to such extremes but it is as well that you are aware of the possibility, so that you are not emotionally crippled if it happens to you. While a hurt can remain, the intensity of emotional upset will fade with time—hence the motto that 'time heals', although personally I prefer to think of it as 'love heals'.

The key point is that moving from one emotion to another happens constantly throughout each day. Negative emotional responses, unless you control them by keeping them in balance and in perspective, can limit your success potential. In other words, unless you control your emotions, they control you.

The symptoms of emotions needing control are when you blow your top over minor incidents or find yourself crying over almost anything you think has gone wrong. This is expected and accepted in very young children but is rarely acceptable behaviour for an adult. At the other extreme, you may have absolute control such that you feel almost nothing. You make no response to external stimuli, even in circumstances where an emotional response might be expected. Some emotions are like those squally summer showers that arrive suddenly and rapidly move on to leave blue skies and sunshine.

Rather than exaggerating or ignoring your emotions it is helpful to take them as they are, to accept them and then to think about and learn from them. After you have found yourself in an unresourceful emotional state, ask these three questions:

1. What was the emotion I felt?
2. What was the emotion telling me about the situation?
3. Why did I experience it then?

So what was the emotion? The clue is found in your body and what it did. A tightening in the stomach or, in extreme situations, a loosening in the bowels or bladder, are pretty good clues that you were experiencing fear; a silly grin and light-headedness are clues to happiness; and tears may be clues to sadness or anger. These are all easily identified but there are more subtle behavioural indicators that help you to name your emotion.

These minor indicators are still body-based behaviour rather than physical reactions. It is possible that an angry expression or a threatening tone of voice indicates the emotion of frustration with the other person, even if you were not previously aware of it. When you learn to make the connection between events and emotions you can understand what triggers them. Noticing the triggers that cause these emotions will allow you the opportunity to respond in a more resourceful manner. (See Chapter 5, Self Success, for tools and techniques to change negative self-talk and limiting beliefs.)

Of course life is rarely as simple as these examples and you may find that there are shades of circumstances. As you consider the second question above, you may find that it was not the situation that provoked your emotion but rather your interpretation of it, even if you misrepresented the facts.

> **SELF DIAGNOSTIC BOX**
>
> When I find myself challenged, how do I react?

Road rage is a modern example of extreme and negative behaviour resulting from an emotional response. Consider the fact or event of someone else cutting you up on the road. You can interpret this as a personal affront and feel anger, or you can interpret it as a novice driver who is doing the best they can with the knowledge and skills available to them and feel a degree of pity. Or you could choose to feel a slight emotion of amusement as you describe the offender to yourself as 'an accident looking for somewhere to happen' and let them go on their way. You feel pleased that they are safely ahead of you rather than in a threatening position tailgating your car. The technique I initially found most effective was to imagine they had an emergency call and were on their way to hospital; it always worked for me. There is one fact (you were cut up) that remains unchanged and here I have presented at least four possible emotional responses which will come into effect according to your interpretation of the event. That is all! Your interpretation will produce the response and you control how you interpret and how you respond. This means you have two opportunities (albeit rapidly passing your consciousness) to control your emotional responses.

Reframing your responses

Reframing is 'changing the scene' by offering yourself an alternative frame. In this way you release yourself from being stuck with the same interpretation of the scene, picture or event and therefore the same response. As in the above example, the driver chooses how to react and usually does this on autopilot. This means that the immediate response is anger or rage. It is at this exact point that the driver had choices—to continue with the rage response or to reframe the whole event by putting a different meaning on it. So put it into a different context or reframe it.

To be effective at reframing you have to identify the circumstances, contexts and situations where you react inappropriately. When you have acknowledged these situations you can prepare your response in advance by reframing. Reframing is simply to change the event by putting another interpretation on it and thus reduce the corresponding negative emotional response.

The six-step process to reduce or diminish stressful situations

1. Sit quietly and mentally recall a situation where you reacted inappropriately. Work on a situation/event that is a recurring scenario for you.
2. Recall the situation as a movie you are in, fully participating as you normally do.
3. NOW! Stop the movie.
4. Change the colours to black and white, turn off any sounds, step outside of the image (so you are looking at it rather than being inside the event—i.e. dissociate) and freeze-frame it so that the movie becomes photographs or still frames.
5. Now think of another similar time you reacted in this inappropriate way and repeat Step 4.
6. Keep doing this until you can experience the event or the thought of the event without an emotional response.

You can use reframing for many different circumstances, for example a bad childhood memory which is holding you back now. Simply repeat the six-step process on the memory until you can remember the event without experiencing any emotional responses. This is a very effective tool for past, present and future inappropriate emotional responses, and it also gives you the freedom to change your interpretation of events.

There is a significant upside to getting in touch with your interpretation patterns as they can reveal some self-defeating and inappropriate behaviour. There are predispositions that may give you clues to the way you react according to your interpretation or view of reality:

1. Black-and-white attitudes with no shades of grey. This is called *dichotomy* where you see events as totally fantastic or absolutely terrible. The truth is rarely found at either of these extremes.

2. *Overt personalisation* where you see another person's reactions as being in direct response to you. If someone is in a bad mood it may be because of something elsewhere in their life and may have nothing to do with you, so don't accept the blame.

3. *Magnified reaction* means that you see an event as having far more impact on your life than it deserves. There is no point in getting emotional over delays on a train or in traffic as the circumstances are beyond your control and rarely really threatening; they are just inconvenient.

4. Remembering adverse circumstances and events to the *exclusion* of the positive ones. For every downside there is always an equal and opposite upside.

SELF DIAGNOSTIC BOX

Have I been guilty of any of these behaviours?

5. Allowing your emotions to flow from *false feelings* or beliefs. If you do something that makes you feel stupid, the false belief would be that 'I am stupid'. You are not. You probably just made a silly mistake but you are far from stupid.

6. Basing a *major decision* on purely emotional factors instead of a critical analysis of the facts, or the pros and the cons of the situation. Your emotions and intuition have parts to play in decision making but they should not assume dominant roles.

For there to be a decision there has to be a multiple choice (even if it is to do something or to do nothing). A choice means that you have power, especially in the way that you respond to your feelings and emotions.

Here are some questions for you to consider about your degree of emotional control.

1. Does the strength or intensity of your emotion match the situation? You would probably experience anger if your car was stolen but, if someone leaves the cap off the toothpaste tube or leaves the toilet seat up, that hardly warrants a show of anger.

2. Do you regularly experience emotions that you need to pay attention to? If happiness eludes you in the mistaken belief that something enjoyable won't last, then you should pay attention to this response and replace it with a better, more resourceful one.

3. What judgements do you frequently make about an event? I recently passed a demolished bus-shelter and overheard an elderly gentleman voice his emotion of disgust at the behaviour of modern youths. His judgement was flawed and his disgust misdirected because the shelter had been demolished by the council to relocate it to a safer position.

4. What are the consequences of your emotionally driven actions? Will they serve you well on your path of success or will they hold you back? How will they impact on other people? Will they move you nearer to your goal or does your emotional response need adjustment?

Please do not allow yourself to become obsessive about analysing your emotions as that is not the objective of this chapter. My aim is to make you aware of some dimensions concerning your emotions that you may not have previously considered and, if you recognised yourself in any of these examples or questions, then you may want to take the appropriate corrective action. If you know that you have a 'short fuse' and react emotionally from habit, try taking a few deep breaths to allow time for the negative emotion to diminish.

If you have been told that you are 'over-emotional' or a 'drama queen' or that you have a 'tendency towards hysteria' because of frequent emotional outbursts, ask yourself what reward you expect from this behaviour. Is it just attention seeking and, heaven forbid, do you actually enjoy the attention that you get from being a victim of circumstances? Being honest with yourself is essential and can be difficult when working with emotions.

You do have a choice. It is better to be a victor than a victim because this opens up your options and gives you freedom for action. You can decide to control how you feel about your circumstances.

Many psychologists specialise in the study of our emotions and this chapter has revealed only the tiniest tip of the iceberg. It has been claimed that as many of these specialists are employed by companies as are employed by the medical disciplines. They are to be found in the marketing and promotional departments and their sole aim is to make products appeal to your emotions rather than your logic.

The cosmetic and perfume industries are especially adept at tugging your emotional strings. By using celebrity endorsements and sexually explicit advertising they are asking you to feel the emotions of desire, sexiness and success by association. Your mix of emotions tells you that if you buy and use these products you will achieve the life of your dreams. If they told you the truth, that you are being charged many pounds for an ounce of a cheap chemical cocktail, produced in a factory and poured into smart bottles with attractive packaging then, unless you are an industrial chemist, your emotions would not be induced.

I deliberately selected perfume for this example as, of all our senses, smell is a powerful emotional trigger. Some supermarkets will claim that their in-store bakery is to ensure that you get fresh bread. This may be true but their real reason is that the smell of freshly baked bread can elicit emotions of gratification, satisfaction, plenty and safety, so you buy a loaf in the anticipation of recapturing those feelings.

Sounds too can trigger emotional responses. Again, one major supermarket chain plays gentle 'new age' music in the vitamin and baby-food aisles to induce a feeling of relaxed well-being. Stirring marches and patriotic music are known to arouse an emotion of pride and patriotic fervour. When the Nimrod movement of Elgar's 'Enigma Variations' is played at a remembrance ceremony it is almost sure to produce a few tears for many listeners.

Visual triggers are created by the careful use of colour. Before their recent change of direction towards healthier food, when a well known fast food outlet was just a burger joint, they used hard surfaces for the chairs (a tactile message) that sloped slightly forward and were in primary red and yellow colours. The intent was to make it really fast food so that you would not want to linger long and thus make room for the next paying customer. When a well known coffee chain went in the opposite direction and introduced muted colours and deep leather sofas they found that people would stay for hours nursing just one cup of coffee.

SELF DIAGNOSTIC BOX

What smells do I love?

SELF DIAGNOSTIC BOX

What music makes me feel happy?

SELF DIAGNOSTIC BOX

What colours do I love?

The mind and body connection

Emotional success and well-being means that you are in touch with your thoughts, feelings and behaviours, that you have learned how to deal with stresses and the problems that arise from time to time and that, generally, you feel good about yourself and feel well. There are many books on the market relating to Emotional Intelligence (EI) or Emotional Intelligence Quotient (EQ) that offer insights into emotional control and some websites offer you the opportunity to measure your EI or EQ. I recommend, as suggested in the Introduction, that you use the RAWPOWER method to explore this further.

When there is emotional imbalance, your body will react to tell you that something isn't right. A good doctor who adopts a holistic approach will always seek to determine a patient's emotional state, especially when any of these symptoms are presented:

* High blood pressure
* Stomach ulcer
* Back pain
* Loss of appetite
* Lethargy
* Insomnia
* Irregular bowels
* Headaches
* Weight changes

These conditions can all be worsened by emotional imbalance or alleviated to a large extent with good emotional well-being. That is not to say that you should ignore any symptoms. Indeed, you should seek qualified medical advice sooner rather than later and as you sit in the waiting room, consider what emotional aspects of your life and lifestyle just might have a bearing on your condition and tell your doctor during the appointment.

Anchoring to aid emotional state control

Anchoring is a process by which any stimulus is connected to, and triggers, a response. Anchors can occur naturally or can be set up intentionally. A common anchor is, 'hear the fire alarm—automatically leave the building', an auditory anchor. 'Alarm' is the anchor and 'leaving the building' is the response triggered by the anchor. A song or a piece of music that reminds you of a certain event is an anchor. When you hear the music you recall the feelings related to the event.

The world of advertising uses the anchoring technique extensively spending billions of pounds creating anchors to good emotional states which make us want to buy a product because we believe we will also get the good emotional state associated with the product. These are unconsciously triggered when we enter shops and they encourage us to buy the advertised products. Anchors are very powerful, which is why they are used in advertising so much and why I am going to show you how to anchor yourself to good emotional states.

Before I do that, let's have a look at some visual anchors that you may be conditioned into using. Traffic signals are a good example of visual anchors that road users recognise and respond to. A person shaking their head from side to side generally means that they are not in agreement with what has been said. Nodding the head up and down is the 'yes I am in agreement' anchor.

An anchor can be anything that will access a response or an emotional state. Anchors can be created in two ways—either by repetition, as in the example of advertising, or through an emotion which has attached itself to a stimulus. Hearing a love song during the first dance you have with a person whom you fall in love with, which reminds you of the dance whenever you hear the song, is an emotional anchor.

In order to anchor states where there are no obvious emotions attached to a stimulus, you can use repetition to create the response. You repeat and repeat the stimulus until the desired response is achieved. This method of anchoring, when used to teach children, is known as learning by rote.

Anchoring of a resourceful emotional state in its simplest form is a seven-step process and once set up can be used to replace negative emotional responses or states.

1. Decide the emotional state that you want to be able to instantly recall, such as feeling confident, composed, self-assured, happy, passionate and so on. I am going to use confidence for this example.

2. Choose the way you want to anchor and recall the emotional state. Some ideas for an anchor are squeezing your earlobe, pinching your index finger and thumb together or pressing the index finger knuckle; you decide. Remember, you may have to do this in public so select something that is acceptable and easy to do and which is not easily noticed.

3. Recall a time when you felt fully confident (this can be recent or from childhood). Remember the event and play it in your mind in full colour, full volume and as an all-action movie of you looking through your own eyes, fully experiencing the state. Spend time with this and make sure you are in the movie, experiencing the state with the noises you would like to hear, the people involved nodding and smiling and you powerfully feeling the state of confidence. Now, turn up the volume, double the feelings and sharpen the colours until your feelings are so acute they are almost tangible.

4. Stop the movie and do something to distract your attention. Stand up, sit down, jump, anything to change your focus for a few seconds. You are clearing the emotional decks so that the next time you run the movie you can anchor it when full emotions are pounding.

5. You are going to associate that state with an anchor or a stimulus. This will allow you to bring back the state whenever you use that stimulus or anchor. I want you to be ready to anchor the feelings when they are fully at peak, and for this example I am going to use squeezing the earlobe. Ready. Steady. Go! Play the movie, full colour, full motion, full sound and add in the full emotional experience of confidence. Double or treble the experience and when you can acutely feel the emotion of confidence, so much so that you nearly overflow with it—at that exact moment—gently squeeze your earlobe for a couple of seconds and release.

6.   Again, stop the movie and do something to distract your attention. Stand up, sit down, jump, anything to change your focus for a few seconds. You are clearing the emotional decks again so that you can check that the anchor you set will work when you squeeze your earlobe.

7.   Squeeze your earlobe as you recall the movie. Now if the anchoring has worked you should have a *rush* or *gush* of the feeling of confidence. Now that it has been anchored you can call this resourceful emotion any time you need it by setting off your anchor (squeezing your earlobe).

If it did not work or only partially worked at number 7 in the above sequence, simply repeat until you are able to feel confident at the triggering of your anchor. The great thing about emotional anchors is they can support you in your journey of emotional control and allow you to concentrate on being successful rather than losing control because your negative emotional responses are taking over.

You can set any number of anchors on all parts of your body and you can also stack anchors which is a very powerful way to evoke more than one emotional response at the same time. This gives extra power to the anchor should you need it. All you do is select the resourceful emotions you would like and anchor them on top of each other using the same anchor point. The stacking of anchors is particularly effective for special events such as a driving test, final exam, public speaking or any event which requires you to really step outside of your normal comfort zone and excel. Good luck and enjoy using anchors.

Everyone has emotions and most emotions are manifest in physical changes or action. The vast majority of people allow their emotions to run on autopilot but a few will experience extremes that indicate an imbalance. If you are aware of a negative recurring emotion that risks becoming a habitual response, then read this chapter again and decide what actions you can take to restore a healthy balance. If you need to employ the services of a professional therapist to assist you with a persistent unresourceful emotional response, go ahead—it is important to overcome this restriction and allow yourself to enjoy a balanced and healthy emotional life. A healthy balance is the key to emotional success.

Success Box

1. Write your list of the emotions that you most often experience

2. List the circumstances or individuals which tend to make you feel these emotions

3. Choose not to let events or individuals determine how you feel—it is your choice, not theirs

4. Stay alert to the inhibiting effects of extreme emotions and the liberating benefits of emotional balance

---

Action I Will Take

Completed on:

/   /

Action I Will Take

Completed on:

/   /

Action I Will Take

Completed on:

/   /

Action I Will Take

Completed on:

/   /

Action I Will Take

Completed on:

/   /

Action I Will Take

Completed on:

/   /

Chapter Five

Self Success

Knowing your strengths, weaknesses, beliefs and values will empower you to have absolute control over your future.

Synopsis

This chapter reveals the secrets of controlling your personal power to be who you want to be, when you want to be.

Josef and Carlo Benrimo were identical twins who were born and lived their childhood in Gibraltar. Although they were identical in appearance, they were poles apart in personality. Josef, who was the elder by some two minutes, grew up to challenge whatever he was told and soon gained a reputation as a difficult teenager. Carlo however, would do all that he could to please everyone around him.

If a parent or teacher told Josef not to do something, he would ask why not. Carlo would say 'OK' and just get on with his peaceful life. The twins achieved very similar grades in their school leaving examinations and it was assumed by their extended families that they would both work in their parents' successful restaurant. Their father, Antonio, suggested that Josef should train to be a cook whilst Carlo could use his happy temperament as front-of-house manager. Antonio hoped that he would be able to retire happily leaving his boys in charge.

Although Josef was headstrong, he had great respect for his father. Even so, he declared that he was going to become famous and that even Gibraltar's most successful restaurant could not offer him the future that he craved. The family discussions were long and difficult for all concerned, but eventually it was agreed that Josef could indeed relocate to Britain whilst Carlo would follow in his father's footsteps.

Both boys are now grown men with families of their own. Carlo inherited the family house and restaurant, simply because that was what was expected of him. But it gradually declined and lost its place as one of the best restaurants on The Rock, all because of his frustration and what he perceived as limitations of parentage, fate and location. This led him to become dissatisfied, then irritable, and eventually he sought his escape in alcohol. His was a classic example of grasping defeat from the jaws of success.

Josef was a free spirit who travelled the world, never accepting that the word 'cannot' would ever apply to him. Indeed, whenever he was told that he couldn't do something he would take it as a challenge and set out to prove the notion wrong. It was this attitude that earned him a place in a televised debate about whether Britain should relinquish sovereignty of his homeland to Spain. His firm stand for the 'against' lobby and his eloquence, despite having had no formal media training, came to the attention of a watching television producer.

Although a career in politics could have been open to him, Josef chose to honour the memory of his father by becoming not a cook, but a chef. He changed his name and is now famous in Britain and the US as one of the first in a long line of celebrity chefs. The brothers were reunited when Josef was the subject of *This is Your Life*. All the participants in the show mentioned his strong self-belief, his confidence and his refusal to accept that there was anything that he could not do if he set his mind on it.

As for Carlo, well Josef used the royalties from his books to buy the freehold of that original family restaurant. He completely refurbished it, promoted it heavily using his assumed name and sent his slightly younger twin to a rehab clinic. Then he gave him the business lock, stock and barrel. If you ever visit Gibraltar you will recognise it by the words carved into the lintel over the front door: 'Believe you can and you will'.

There are many facets to our personalities and the amazing mixture that makes us who we are. This chapter will not delve into deep psychological theories or behavioural science. Instead it reveals some insights into the 'what' and 'whys' of your behaviours and how these colour the results that you create in your life. You will also discover some powerful tools and techniques for taking control of your life and destiny. We will be looking at your beliefs, values, self-esteem, confidence, personal development and understanding.

Who are you?

You get to choose this and have already chosen your life so far. This might be a bit of a hard pill to swallow as we have often been taught to give the responsibility of our lives to others. We learn the apparent effectiveness of the illusion of a blame culture at a young age and, sadly, we also learn dependency. You only have to look around you at the media to see that every day the 'government' should be doing something about it! Not you, not I, not the victims or perpetrators, just 'the government' or worse, an undefined 'they'. Until and unless you decide to take back the total responsibility for your successes and failures you will never feel successful.

You may have all the trappings of modern day material success—the luxury car, a big house, designer clothes and expensive holidays—but you will always feel that there is something missing. Some of my 'successful' clients have expressed the fear that, some day, they will get the tap on the shoulder that they have been dreading—the one which says 'you have been found out as a fraudster'. This is because they lack real inner self-belief and avoid taking full responsibility for their own lives. Others who appeared to 'have it all' have confessed to the anti-climactic feeling described as 'is that it then?'

Your self-image is the accumulation of every attitude and opinion that you have ever been told about yourself since birth. You have perpetuated and reinforced this by repetition until eventually it has formed the subconscious picture of your self-image. This has become who you believe you are; it determines how you respond to life and what you believe you are capable of doing. It has become your comfort zone.

This comfort zone is the life that you are comfortable living, although it could be full of pain, poverty and drudgery. People remain in these situations because their self-image and belief systems support them there. They feel secure and comfortable in the knowledge that this is what they deserve or all that they are worthy of.

You are within a closed loop. Your self-image is created by your belief system (what you believe to be true about yourself). You build and nourish these beliefs and feel comfortable with them. They become who you believe you are. You know and trust them because you can prove that they are right and, therefore, they must be true. You have images of yourself in different contexts and you tell yourself how to perform and then reinforce the results of the performance with self-talk.

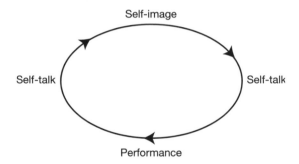

This example demonstrates the steps:

1. You believe you cannot dance.
2. You have a visual picture of not being able to dance.
3. You confirm verbally (also, inside your head) when asked to dance: 'I cannot dance.'
4. You begin to dance.
5. You fail (fall over, trip, step on toes etc.).
6. You reconfirm verbally (again, inside your head): 'There! I told you I was no good at dancing!'
7. You reinforce the negative self-image.
8. You continue to repeat the cycle.

Every time you repeat these steps you make your belief stronger. It is called adding references to the belief. In this context, references can be any supporting actions, words, attitudes or thoughts that confirm your belief, even if it was a false belief from the outset.

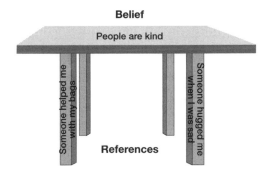

How does it work? Well, think of a table top (your belief) without any table legs (references). It would not be able to stand up and therefore it would not exist as a table (not a belief—just an idea). Now, if you fix one leg (reference) onto the table top you now have a wobbly table (weak belief). Fix 20 legs (references) to your table top (belief) and you now have a very strong table (belief).

The great thing about this analogy is that it is easy to dismantle a table and create another one. The same can be true of dismantling a belief; all you need is to believe that you can do it. Use the method described below and remember, if you decide that you can change your old limiting belief, you will be right.

It is well worth remembering that some of your current self-beliefs have come from other people and the things they have told you. Those other people could have been your parents and close relatives when you were a child. Later they may have been your friends, teachers, bosses or even total strangers. They probably gave you at least a hundred 'negative strokes' for every one 'great stroke' and, even if they were delivered with good intent, they were based on those individuals' opinions. Remind yourself that opinions belong to others and that it is wrong to take what isn't yours. This is especially true in the context of beliefs that can, all too often, become self-fulfilling prophecies.

Belief change

A strong motivator for changing a belief is to decide which limiting belief you want to change and then to ask yourself, 'What has this belief cost me?'

1. What has it cost me to keep this belief on a personal level?
2. What has it cost me to keep this belief on a professional level?
3. What has it cost me to keep this belief on a financial level?

Now decide what you would like to believe instead. The replacement belief needs to be stated positively; this means without any negatives within the statement of belief.

SELF DIAGNOSTIC BOX

What has my negative belief cost me so far?

Create a belief statement consisting of four **P**s:

P	You must state your new belief in *Personal* terms—this means that it belongs to you	I
P	Must be stated in the *Present* tense—as if it has already happened	Am
P	Must be *Powerfully* stated—to give it some passion and oomph!	Brilliant
P	Must be *Positive*—only use positive words	At Maths

You need to replace the original belief with a new belief that is stated in personal, present tense, powerful and positive terms. If, for instance, you wanted to give up smoking, you would not include the word 'smoking' as that is the negative you wish to remove. So avoid saying 'I am a non-smoker' as there are two negatives in this statement: the word 'non' and the word 'smoker'.

In this example, you would need to think about what you really want to be, to have or to do. Some of my clients have successfully used, 'I have clean and healthy lungs', 'I live a healthy life',

'I respect my lungs' and 'I breathe clean air'. I am sure you get the idea. All you need to do is to decide on a statement to replace the limiting/negative belief.

Here are a few more examples of empowering beliefs:

- I am a fantastic cook
- I am a calm person
- I am a brilliant mathematician
- I feel terrific
- I am outstanding at golf
- I am a remarkable letter writer
- I am a great football player
- I am a very clever person
- I am fabulously happy
- I am a great speller
- I am happy ironing
- I am an amazing public speaker

When you have your new belief statement, see yourself performing that task as you wish to perform it.

About now, your logical conscious mind will take any of those belief statements and may well produce the thought, 'Oh yeah? Pull the other one, it's got bells on!' Your less dominant subconscious mind is many times more powerful than your conscious mind. It has another attribute in that it is absolutely incapable of criticising or judging; it just accepts whatever you feed into it and then attempts to make it happen. To access this powerful part of your mind you need to silence the constant chatter of logical thoughts and allow the subconscious to make your new belief a reality.

An effective way to do this is through visualisation.

Visualise the belief

Create a full colour, full volume, action movie of you successfully performing. Spend time with this and make sure you are in the movie, experiencing the performance with the noises you would like to hear, the people involved encouraging and applauding and you feeling confident that you are performing successfully. Add in some smells and tastes to the movie if applicable as this will involve all your five senses and make the experience feel real.

Once you have perfected your mental movie add in your new four **Ps** belief statement and repeat it as you play it back in your head. When you have both the movie and the new belief coupled and working in a synchronised way, you can now really

SELF DIAGNOSTIC BOX

What do I consistently visualise?

have some fun. When you 'play' your movie, increase all your senses by 20 per cent, turn up your feelings, increase your sounds, sharpen the colours, smell the smells and taste success.

Get the phizzyology (physiology)

This means that you need to change your body posture when working on limiting beliefs. When you think or talk about your limiting belief you hold yourself in a certain way. Let me explain. Think of a time in your life when you were sad about something— do this for a couple of minutes until you recapture the experience. Notice how you hold your head, where your eyes are looking, how you hold your facial features. What is your neck and what are your shoulders doing? What has happened to your spine? Where are your feet placed during this recall? How are you breathing? Stop as soon as you have become fully aware of your phizzyology.

Now, remember a time when you were so excited and happy you were jumping up and down. (If you cannot remember then imagine you have won £25,000,000 on the lottery.) Really get into this state, fully enjoy the experience and jump up and down if you can. Laugh out loud and smile until your face hurts. Notice how you hold your head, where your eyes are looking, how you hold your facial features. What is your neck and what are your shoulders doing? What has happened to your spine? Where are your feet during all this excitement? How are you breathing? You hold your head up, have a straight back, look up or look forward and your facial muscles will be forming a smile. That is changing your phizzyology.

The great thing about this technique is that it shows you how you can change your feelings and thoughts simply by moving your body into a more resourceful position. It is hard to be depressed with your head held high and a smile on your face. Now while you have the phizzyology of happiness, add it into the movie you have created for your new empowering belief. Once you have managed to do this, continue to increase all these sensations (visual, sounds, feelings, tastes and smells) and keep increasing until you have a movie that, when you run it from start to finish, changes the way you feel and think about yourself and weakens or destroys the limiting belief.

Well done! It is now time to put all you know into regular use until it becomes a habit and then a new belief.

New empowering belief embodiment

I will again use the steps for a limiting negative belief with 'I cannot dance' as an example.

1. You find yourself saying and believing: 'I cannot dance.' (SELF-IMAGE)

2. As soon as you say or think it, shout aloud or in your head: 'STOP—DELETE THIS THOUGHT NOW!'

3. Play your new empowering movie of you being able to dance.

4. DECIDE TO POSITIVE SELF-TALK. You confirm verbally (also, inside your head): 'I am a fantastic dancer.'

5. You go to a dance (PERFORMANCE), enjoy dancing and if you need to have dancing lessons—book them!

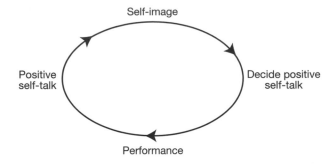

Self-image

Positive
self-talk

Decide positive
self-talk

Performance

6. You reconfirm verbally (again, inside your head): 'There! I am fantastic at dancing!'

7. POSITIVE SELF-TALK. Reinforced self-image.

8. Repeat this cycle every time you think about dancing.

Now you *can* believe this will be an *easy* process and *will* work for you every time. Some of you will want to believe that you need to work hard to change beliefs and need to book some training, read books, hire a coach or mentor, and that is fine. If you need to change the wording a little to 'My dancing is always improving' then that is OK. Taking action is the key.

Remember that *you* are the one holding on to and reinforcing the belief. *You* and *you alone* hold your limiting beliefs and therefore *you* can choose to release yourself from them. All it takes is the decision that *you* will no longer settle for less. Go for it!

> **SELF DIAGNOSTIC BOX**
> **What limiting belief am I going to change?**

What are your values?

We may hear a lot about values and yet we rarely take the time to decide exactly what our own values are and the impact they are having on our decisions and lifestyle. Simply put, values are elements that are important to you in life. Most people when asked this question will answer with a tangible and materialistic response, such as an item from the list below:

- Family
- iPod
- Golf
- Career
- Friends
- TV
- Money
- Pets
- House
- Car
- Clothes
- Holiday
- Partner
- Bling
- Yacht

These things may well be important to you but they are not values simply because you can touch them. A value is most easily described as intangible—something that you cannot touch. Therefore, the list above does not fit the category. They are the means to the value. What you gain from each of the tangibles in your life and that you hold so dearly will lead you to your values.

Here's what you can do. Ask yourself the same question until you have at least eight different answers.

What is important to me in life?	
What else is important to me in life?	
What else is important to me in life?	
What else is important to me in life?	

What else is important to me in life?	
What else is important to me in life?	
What else is important to me in life?	
What else is important to me in life?	

Your values chart may have a combination of tangible and non-tangible words and that is OK at this stage. Your chart could look something like this.

An example of a values chart

What is important to me in life?	Money (tangible)
What else is important to me in life?	Security
What else is important to me in life?	Family (tangible)
What else is important to me in life?	Love
What else is important to me in life?	Holidays (tangible)
What else is important to me in life?	Fulfilment
What else is important to me in life?	Peace
What else is important to me in life?	Sailing (tangible)

Now go back over the answers and ask: 'Can I touch this?' If the answer is 'Yes', ask yourself, 'What does this mean to me?' or 'What does this give me?' until you have a word which is non-tangible.

Here is a list of some non-tangible values my clients have discovered:

- Love
- Courage
- Integrity
- Contribution
- Peace
- Faith
- Equality
- Ethics
- Fulfilment
- Honesty
- Freedom
- Sincerity
- Success
- Respect
- Independence
- Security
- Happiness
- Dignity
- Achievement
- Enthusiasm

Remember we are looking for a non-tangible word and it may help to ask yourself one of the following: 'Is this absolute for me?', 'Is this ultimate for me?' or 'Is this unquestionable for me?' By asking this extra question you are testing the answer to ensure that you really believe it is wholly true for you and not just a value you have adopted. It is important to understand that sometimes a tangible response (family) may represent more than one value for you, such as love, happiness and security. In this instance you simply write all the values associated with the tangible word. You may find this activity easier if you work with someone outside of your immediate friends and family group, where they simply ask you the questions and write down your answers. It needs to be a person that you do not feel the need to impress as this will alter your responses, and your replies need to be honest and accurate for you to truly benefit from the activity.

Once you have your list of values, put them in order of importance—and the quickest way to do that is to give each value a mark. If you have eight values you have the numbers 1 to 8 to allocate. Read your list and ask yourself: 'Which one of these has the most power?' or 'Which is the most important to me?' and then work down the list. If you hear conflicting messages, listen to your intuition because for this exercise you need the most influential and truthful response. When you have your values in the order of importance you will know what influences your decision making.

I had a client who was employed as a sales director with responsibility for a sales team. He was employed on a commission-based salary. When we worked together he mentioned that he had it all: a lovely family, a great job, a fantastic car and a large impressive house, and yet he always felt unhappy and stressed. To everyone looking at his life from the outside, he appeared to be a successful man but on the inside he was unfulfilled and unhappy.

Once we had uncovered his values and put them into the order of importance to him, we discovered that his top value was security! Think about the implications of this result in the light of his position at work. No wonder he felt unhappy and stressed—his income each month was not secure because it was dependent on the sales team reaching its targets! Therefore his income was totally dependent on other people—a double whammy for insecurity.

Once he understood the influence that his values had on his decisions and his life, he was able to negotiate a guaranteed basic salary to cover his regular financial commitments plus a commission-based bonus to ensure he kept his team up to the mark.

When you know your values, you have a vital edge when making important decisions. Simply run the options against your values list and, if by selecting the choice the result is that you match your values, you will be happy. If your top values are compromised it would be advisable to select another option.

Self-acceptance

One of the keys to being successful is to accept yourself as you are now. Acceptance is the cornerstone of self-confidence. If you accept that self-confidence is easy and know that you are absolutely right the result will be self-confidence. Easy!

However, many spend their lives comparing themselves with others and emphasising their own lack. This is not only an absolute waste of time, it is harmful to self-confidence as there will always be people who have more skills, knowledge, talents, advantages and qualities than you. So STOP doing this to yourself.

To improve your life and take action you need to take stock of where you are now. If you find that where you are now is not a good place to be, you must accept yourself and the current situation in order to know exactly what needs to be done.

I often use a little phrase when I become aware that I have a negative thought. I say to myself, 'I love and accept myself and release the … into the universe.' I also use the following question when I want to move forward from an uncomfortable position that I have created for myself: 'How many rules do I need to have in place before I can praise my achievements?'

Now, ask yourself the same question.

SELF DIAGNOSTIC BOX

How many rules do I need to have in place before I can praise my achievements?

The staggering answer to this question is usually 'many'. Most of us decide that many things have to happen (sometimes in a special sequence) before we believe we are successful, loved, beautiful, happy or whatever. Pick one of these and be honest with yourself as you ask the question.

Write your answers down so that you can really see the difficulties you place in your own path. For example:

'What needs to happen before I feel loved?'

- I need to be 20 per cent slimmer
- I need to have 20,000 (GBP, USD, EUR, HKD, JYP etc.) in the bank
- I need to drive a Porsche 911
- I need to wear designer clothes
- I need to be a fully qualified
- I need to be blonde
- My husband must love me

These replies are all nonsensical self-delusions. You must fully accept that you are the one making the rules and you are the one adhering to them. Think about this now for a few minutes. How hard are YOU making your life?

Here are some alternative rules for what feeling loved could be, if you would only let it be.

'What could I choose to happen so that I feel loved?'

- When the sun shines
- When I wake up in the morning
- When it rains
- When a neighbour says, 'Hello'
- When anyone asks me, 'How are you today?'
- When my pet brushes past my legs
- When I make someone smile
- When I listen to music
- When I breathe
- When I laugh

> **SELF DIAGNOSTIC BOX**
>
> What do I need to have happen to feel happy?

The list could, and should, be endless if you want to live a successful life in your model of the world.

Just to really put this into perspective ask yourself the following question: 'What needs to happen to make me feel I have been a disappointment?'

Yes, you guessed—not much! You probably only have one rule or one thing that has to happen to make you feel disappointed or a failure. Often it will be the actions of your boss, your partner, your parents or your colleagues.

WAKE UP!

You are responsible for making your life difficult and you can make your life easy. You are the one who is making ludicrous rules by which you have to live and then you inflict these rules on your life. Give yourself and those who love you a break!

Decide now to live by easier rules. Whenever you find yourself talking rubbish or thinking negative things about yourself, use the STOP strategy and run a different sentence that empowers you. Only you can do this. Only you can decide now to put this into effect. Only *you* can change *you*. Whenever you feel the desire to do something ask: 'What is it that drives me to want this?'

There are a few essential things that drive us to take actions.

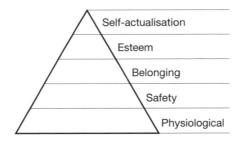

Abraham Maslow's Hierarchy of Needs, 1943

In 1943, Abraham Maslow wrote a paper titled *A Theory of Human Motivation*, where he hypothesised that we all have fundamental needs which fall into a hierarchal dependency. In other words, that we need to have our physiological needs in place before we can consider our safety needs, and our safety needs in place before we will satisfy our belonging needs, our belonging needs before our esteem needs, and only when we have all the four fundamental needs satisfied will we ever reach self-actualisation.

The needs in brief

- Physiological needs are breathing, water, food, sleep, sex
- Safety needs are security and feeling safe, health and well-being
- Belonging needs are love, friendships, family or extended family support, spiritual frameworks
- Esteem means being respected and having self-respect and recognition
- Self-actualisation is the instinctive need to be the best we can be, to grow, to develop, to learn

An easier way of looking at these is to ask which ones you need to be satisfied.

1. To satisfy a body function
2. To feel sure of myself, secure, safe and well
3. To feel loved, cared for
4. To feel important (needed, respected), to be one of the gang
5. To have diversity and challenges

If you are aware of the need level you are working from, you will have an insight into the drivers affecting your decisions and will be able to adjust to accommodate—and therefore get the optimum results.

The key message of this chapter is that you are the keeper of your own destiny, your own happiness and your own feelings of well-being. When would *now*, be a good time to take action and make your life outstanding?

Success Box

1. Write down one of your limiting beliefs

2. How much has this belief cost you personally, professionally and financially?

3. Write a four Ps statement

4. Decide now to take control of your thoughts

5. Write your core values in order of importance

Action I Will Take

Completed on:

/   /

Action I Will Take

Completed on:

/   /

Action I Will Take

Completed on:

/   /

Action I Will Take

Completed on:

/   /

Action I Will Take

Completed on:

/   /

Action I Will Take

Completed on:

/   /

Chapter Six

Financial Success

Buy what you want when you want it.

Synopsis

Ways of dealing with debt, your financial workout, how to invest for financial success and how to keep it from fraudsters.

Theresa Gertrude O'Malley had always had a dream of visiting New York. She had struggled all her life to ensure that her children were well fed, clean and polite, even if their clothes were repaired often and handed down to their younger siblings. She had married young to her childhood sweetheart who was several years older than her. Patrick had passed away. Now, physically frail but in full command of her mental faculties, she was spending her twilight years in a warden assisted apartment. This allowed her to retain her pride and independence, with the security of knowing that there was always someone on call in the building if a crisis arose.

Because her three children had joined the armed forces, from their own choice, it seemed a cruel twist of fate that two had made the ultimate sacrifice for their country. Theresa Gertrude O'Malley was looking forward to her birthday the following week. Her library book fell to her lap as she went to sleep with a contented smile, thinking that her youngest daughter, Bernadette, would soon be visiting to help her celebrate. Bernadette arrived a day early. She carried an empty suitcase and waved an envelope at her mum. Despite having lived in London for many years, she still had an Irish lilt to her voice as she said, 'Get packing, we're off for a week in New York tomorrow. It is all booked and paid for and we will be travelling first class all the way to our five star hotel in Times Square.'

The old lady had a suspicious glint in her eye. 'And how, did you pay for it? If it was on one of those blessed credit card things, I am not going and neither will you! If you expect me to thank you for getting into debt and wasting money you can't afford, then you had better think again.' Bernie tossed her long auburn hair and, with a twinkle in her eyes said, 'Relax Mum, I did it all with your little brown envelopes. Just like you used to do, every month I put aside the money I needed for my outgoings and a little aside for this trip. I did not have brown envelopes like you used when we were kids but instead I put my savings into the bank. The result is the same in that I had some money to spare for this birthday trip.'

Theresa Gertrude O'Malley, reclined her seat and allowed her eyes to close. As she drifted into a happy sleep, the words security and independence were repeating over and over in her mind. If only her beloved Patrick knew, he would be proud for them both and for Bernadette's financial success. But maybe he did know?

What does financial success mean? This will depend on your circumstances at the time of asking. For some people it means getting out of debt and having money left over at the end of the week. For others it means owning a private jet and a limousine. For others it means celebrity status. What is truly important is for you to decide what financial success means to you. Before you can answer that question you need to identify your exact financial position now.

> **SELF DIAGNOSTIC BOX**
>
> **What does financial success mean to me?**

Monthly outgoings

Do you know exactly what you spend or exactly what your outgoings are per month? Without this knowledge you will have no clear understanding of your finances and, instead of creating success, will have to trust to luck.

The table below is a guideline for you to work out where you are now. The only rule is to be honest because your future success is built on absolute honesty. If you have debts you must be honest about them.

Outgoing description	Amount per month £
Residence costs – mortgage or rental payments	
Sustenance – food, household products, pet food etc.	
Utilities – gas, electric, water, phones (including mobiles) etc.	
Local tax – community, council etc. If income tax and national insurance are not deducted from your pay at source record them here	
Travel costs (public) – train, plane, bus, underground etc.	
Travel costs (private) – car or motor bike, car/ bike loan or leasing, fuel, MOT, repairs, tax, services, cleaning, parking etc.	
Clothes – all forms of clothing including shoes, uniforms, work overalls, suits, casual, sports, dry cleaning etc.	
Insurances – household, car, life, disability and serious illness, pets etc.	
Pension provisions – pension payments	
Other household expenses – home and garden tools, repairs, replacements, supplies, furniture, furnishings etc.	
Debt repayments – credit cards, store cards, personal loans from friends and family, bank loans, study loans (unless already included above), bank charges etc.	

Outgoing description	Amount per month £
Personal expenses – haircuts/styling, nails, massage, therapies, make-up, gymnasium etc.	
Children – specific child expenses such as nursery, nanny, babysitting, school/university fees, pocket money, school trips etc.	
Entertainment – films, DVDs, music, shows, restaurant/take-away meals, bars, books, seminars, social events, all TV costs, dance/ evening classes, broadband, boats, hobbies etc.	
Projects – building an extension, conservatory, garden designs, kitchen etc.	
Contribution to society – charities, governor groups, parents' associations, church, synagogue, mosque, temple etc.	
Holidays – annual holiday, weekenders, visits to family etc. (remember to break this down to monthly costs)	
Investments – monthly life policies, bonds, ISAs, any investments etc.	
Extra expenses – anything you buy not included above such as lunch (workdays), newspapers, drinks, lottery, birthdays, Christmas, gambling etc.	
Total monthly expenditure	

Well done if you completed this task! I know how just getting this information together can be a challenge if you have never done it before. Apart from the time and effort involved, there is the emotional aspect of fear for some people who, until now, figured they would somehow muddle through as they always have before and would rather hide from the truth. Yet almost as many are happily surprised at the result as those who are somewhat concerned.

The good news is that you only need to do the whole thing once; then you can update it monthly or, if you have a very stable life-style, whenever anything significant changes. If you have found that your outgoings are more than your incomings, you must plan and take some drastic action to restore the balance. There are two areas for consideration here. The fastest way is to look at each item in the list above and see how you can cut back on either the cost or frequency of each spend. You could also explore the options for increasing your income by changing jobs, working additional overtime or turning a hobby into a profitable business sideline.

Fifteen tips for saving money

1. Shop online at comparison sites to get the best deals for everything.

2. Set up direct debits for regular payments to avoid extra charges.

3. Research the possibility of having a water meter installed and do a price comparison of the prices you would have paid in the last 12 months with and without a water meter. This way you can make your decision based on the figures. If you live alone or with one other, and you are not metered, you will be paying the same as a large family and you may find the meter system a cheaper alternative.

4. Have an interest paying current account and shop around for the best rates.

5. Pay off your credit cards at the end of each month. If you set up direct debits you will avoid paying high interest charges and it will become a true credit card rather than a 'debt card', which it is for most people. Remember you are never in credit with a 'balance' on these cards. You are always in debt as soon as you slip past the interest-free periods.

6. Turn off all electrical goods and lights when you are not using them. This means all and any appliances as several appliances left on standby can increase your energy costs alarmingly.

7. Have a look at your entertainment expenditure and find ways of cutting back. If you go to a restaurant every week consider going fortnightly or finding a cheaper place to go. Every penny saved will be a penny for your future financial success.

8. If your budget is high and your holiday costs are also high then this is an area you could temporarily cut back on for the next couple of years or until you have a financial budget that is able to accommodate trips. Consider talking to your family or friends about sharing holidays or staying with your family for a break.

9. Stop buying lunches and 'designer coffees'. Prepare a packed lunch and take that with you.

10. If you buy a newspaper every day, break the habit and get your news from the internet or listen to the radio. If your paper is just for something to read on the journey into work, go to the library and borrow a book, perhaps one on money management.

SELF DIAGNOSTIC BOX

What savings in my monthly expenditure can I make now?

11. Look at your personal expenditure and if you are visiting an expensive hairdresser, find one who has left the salon and set up a mobile practice. Then you will be paying for the cut and not subsidising the overheads of the salon.

12. Cancel your private gymnasium membership and go to a local authority gym. They are usually as well equipped with fees at half the cost of a private gym. Or, do as I did, and find a sport which does not need to be financed every month.

13. Ideally seek independent professional financial advice to consider organising a flexible debt repayment scheme for all your

credit, loan and current debt. Remember you need to do this in line with your outgoings. Remember to reduce costs wherever you can and do not purchase anything outside of your budget no matter what happens.

14. Sort out all the stuff you have not used in the last two years and sell it. Sell all your unwanted goods at boot sales or on the internet. There are buyers for most things.

15. Always carefully check your bank and credit card statements every month to ensure all the transactions belong to you. Mistakes happen, as does fraud, and it is your responsibility to contain this.

Do you know your net worth?

Do you even know what net worth means? Well done if you can answer 'yes' to this question. The chances will be that you already have investment plans and strategies in place.

Net worth is the difference between *all* your assets and *all* your liabilities. In other words, if you were to sell everything you own (and I do mean everything!) and paid off everything you owe, then your net worth is what is left in your bank or pocket.

American businessman and property developer, Donald Trump, who is allegedly worth hundreds of millions of dollars, is reported to have commented, when passing a tramp begging on the streets of Manhattan, 'That man probably has a greater net worth than I have.' His remark was from his acute awareness that, at the time he is purported to have said this, his property empire was mortgaged several times over. His 'wealth' was an illusion based on debt.

For simplicity here, your net worth is what you have when you have calculated all of your assets and taken away all of your liabilities. Also, I have separated out some of the assets to enable you to have a clear picture of your finances. Let's do it!

No	Description	Value/ Amount £
1	**Fixed assets** – items difficult to sell quickly Property owned – *not your home* (market value minus outstanding related debts) Business collateral Specialised collections, art, stamps, classic cars, memorabilia etc. Other	
	Total of fixed assets	
2	**Liquid assets** – items easy or quick to sell (not money or cash) Pensions Life insurance PEPs, ISAs, Stocks, shares, bonds etc. Endowment policies (resale value not surrender value) Long term savings (notice needed for withdrawal) Collections, art, stamps, memorabilia etc.	
	Total of liquid assets	
3	**Money** – cash or savings Bank accounts Saving accounts (instant withdrawal) Cash Other cash equivalents	
	Total of money	
4	**Home** – current market value of your home minus any related debts (mortgage)	
	Total of home	
5	**Possessions** – personal belongings of value Jewellery, musical instruments, vehicles, bikes, electrical goods etc.	
	Total of possessions	
	Add the totals from 1 to 5 = total of assets	

Please note that money is a liquid asset. To make it easier for you to get a clear picture of your personal finances, I have separated money from the other liquid assets because you can have immediate access to it.

Now we need to have a look at your liabilities—these are what you owe to other people.

No	Description	Value/ Amount £
1	Outstanding amount on mortgages (other than allowed for in 4 above)	
2	Credit card debts	
3	Store card debts	
4	Other loans (include hire purchase and leasing agreements)	
5	Business loans	
6	Student loans	
7	Other debts	
	Total of liabilities	

Now that you know your liabilities and your assets, you can calculate your net worth.

Calculation	Net worth
Total of assets minus total of liabilities	

Well done if you have completed these tasks. It can be hard work but it will be time well spent because your potential permanent gain will be many times greater than any temporary pain. I hope that the net worth figures are positive for you.

Remember that even if you are in a negative net worth position at the moment, this does not mean that you will always be in that situation. I would recommend that you make an appointment with your bank manager or an independent financial advisor, with the aim of working on a debt recovery programme. Then you can stop worrying, start taking control and then concentrate on planning your future financial success and security.

If you are already in a positive net worth situation, you might like to examine the returns you are getting on your investments. Have you recently compared these percentages in relation to the national average returns and the top rate of returns? Many people set up investments and then rarely check them. There are two good reasons to revisit them:

1. The performance of your investment may not be keeping up with the current marketplace and it may be worth moving your money.
2. Your own attitude to risk may have changed and therefore you might look at the investments in a different light.

Why not use the chart opposite to assess your current attitude to risk.

Most knowledgeable investors will 'spread their bets', which means having a little bit of the total in three or more areas. This method protects some of the money from total loss and simultaneously allows some of the money to grow exponentially. The overall returns are likely to come out around the medium to high on a bull market (good market which is growing and prices are going up) and medium to low in a bear market (poor market where the prices are coming down).

One of the greatest pieces of advice I was given when I had my first bonus payment was to split it over three risk money chests.

Low risk   Medium risk   **High risk**

Your attitude to risk	Investment return	Financial investment	Investment in property, including building projects	% return example
Very high	Double your money or more	Futures or options market	Land planning application	40–400
High	Not as high	Adventurous fund / emerging market	Property development project	25–55
Medium	Medium	Managed fund	Property conversion	12–35
Cautious	Low to medium	Bond	Simple renovation project	5–25
Very cautious	Low	Fixed interest	Buying a repossessed house in good condition priced below the market rate	5–10

I divided my bonus by three and put an equal share into a low risk, medium risk and a high risk investment. This is an example of 'spreading my bet' because I spread the money and the risk at the same time. I do this with all windfalls or unexpected income, probably because I like a little flutter and do not like losing hard earned money. It gives me the best of both worlds—some security and a little gamble.

Income generation

So far we have been discussing what you have and how to invest it. Now we are going to look at some ways to earn money. If your definition of financial success means having a significantly large income, then you will probably need more than a salary to generate it. Your thoughts will turn to multiple streams of income where the money derives from different sources. Most seriously rich people have multiple streams of income and so do many companies.

In Britain, it is difficult to talk to anyone about success and wealth for very long before Richard Branson is mentioned. His Virgin Group includes trains, planes, media, retail, publishing, soft drinks, spirits, mobile phones, satellite TV, radio, holidays, banking and, by the time these pages are published, he will probably have come up with even more areas to invest in. If multiple streams of income are good enough for Richard Branson, they sure are good enough for me.

The question is, how can I do this? Well, as I mentioned in Chapter One, you start from where you are and make a plan. Here are some ideas of the frameworks for multiple streams of income, but you will need to do your research to select which will suit you and how you are going to make it happen.

Here are the some definitions of income under the multiple streams banner. I have left space at the bottom for your own ideas or others you have heard about.

Money generator	Have it already ✓	Amount generated per annum £
Main employment		
Second job		
Owner of small business		
Shareholder in small business		
Property investments		
Stocks and shares investments		
Multi-level marketing product		
Internet website with a membership area		
Internet website with products		
Write a book or an e-book		
Affiliate marketing (selling other people's products on your website or linking an affiliate programme to their website)		
Speaking or training in your area of expertise		
Produce CDs and/or MP3s on your specialist subjects		

Now you need to decide which one you are going to do next. What do you need to do to get started on this income stream? Make a list of the steps involved and start taking action. Before you know it you will have another income and, once you have one going, you can start another.

Active and passive

The main thrust of this entire book is about you taking responsibility for your own success and this inevitably means that you have to take action. Let me swerve away from that theme for a moment by suggesting that there is at least one instance where 'passive' is best.

No matter how hard you work, there are only so many hours, days, weeks and months when you can keep going. This, of course, imposes a limit on your potential wage, salary or earnings. I have already mentioned investments where, once you have taken the initial action, if you have chosen wisely, your wealth will increase with no further effort on your part. This presents a slight snag in that if you decide you want to enjoy the fruits of your wisdom, you will have to sell your shares or other investments in exchange for real cash. So you will have your pleasure but you will no longer have that particular wealth generator.

Many millionaires were created during the 1920s and early 1930s when the insurance industry was booming because all manner of products were targeted at people who, hitherto, had been unable to afford even a few pennies a week. Now pennies do add up into pounds. The early insurance salesmen would earn a very modest commission from each sale and this met their immediate family needs for food and shelter. Those who made millions did so by taking an even smaller commission! They did so in return for a 'residual' commission of a small percentage of each annual renewal premium paid by their clients. Don't bother even trying to do the maths, but just imagine 100 new clients a year, each paying an annual premium for up to 40 years and the salesman gets his cut each and every time. Some of them 'retired' from selling after just a few years on the road and built vast fortunes from this residual, passive income.

Passive income is money that flows into your account whether you are awake or asleep, at home or on holiday, working nine to five or even writing a book. The Internet is now creating passive incomes for many entrepreneurs around the world.

Protect what you have

Once you have control of your finances you need to protect them from fraud. Reports in the media have stated that one in four people in the UK either know a victim or have themselves been affected by some form of identity theft. It can take 300 hours or more to clear your name and reputation if someone commits fraud in your name. This cost in time, loss of earnings and sheer inconvenience should be enough for you to take notice. Add the damage to your credit rating, the possible freezing of bank accounts and the embarrassment of bouncing cheques, to give you a few compelling reasons to take some action to protect your finances.

Ten ways to add layers of protection

1. Shred! Buy a diamond shredder and use it on anything that has your name, address, telephone number, banking details and any personal information. This also includes unsolicited junk mail offering credit cards because thieves will steal these and then apply on the forms, which are pre-printed with your details.

2. Buy a safe or a lockable cabinet, hide it somewhere secret in your home and store all personal documents in it.

3. Be vigilant with your post. If you have applied for a credit card or other facility put a reminder for yourself to check that it has arrived within a few days and, if you have not received it, call the supplier and tell them, as it could have been intercepted in the mail. It is estimated that some 14 million items of mail are lost every year. If you live in a property where other people have access to the mail be extra vigilant.

4. Develop a phone phobia around your personal information. Never give any personal details over the phone unless you have checked the legitimacy of the person and the phone number and preferably dialled their number yourself for authentication. Never give out your full pin number as reputable organisations will never seek it. Be aware of who is listening, especially if you are using a mobile phone.

5. Be very cautious with emails purporting to come from a bank which asks you to fill in a form for any reason whatsoever. Never reply. If you think it *could* be genuine, telephone your bank (don't just hit 'reply' on your email!) and check before responding.

6. Never respond to telephone calls or emails that state that you are a 'winner'. If you have not entered a competition or draw you cannot possibly be a winner, so it will always be a scam. If you have to pay an administration or other charge to receive your winning prize this is definitely a scam and you should report it to the police.

7. Passwords and pin numbers need to be different. Keep your banking password different from all other passwords, never write it down and never keep it (or your PIN number) with bank cards.

8. Take care if you are offered an investment which seems too good to be true. If the returns are much higher than expected and the marketing hype is glossy be extra vigilant. Do due diligence and research the investment. Avoid the investment unless every claim can be verified.

9. When you speak to a financial advisor you need to know the costs involved and whether they are truly independent. What are the charges and how will you be expected to pay? Be alert if you are told the charges come from the investments—ask what happens if there is a market downturn. Ask what percentage of your investment the financial advisor will get and if there are annual management and maintenance charges and how much these would be.

10. Always ask the costs of cancellation or opting out of any investment, mortgage or other financial deal. Some companies have low charges to get you and your money on board, then impose punitive penalties if you want to move on.

We have covered many things in this chapter at a 'big picture' level and this means that you now have some ideas and need to find ways to take your ideas forward. You have a process for finding your net worth and you have a platform to build upon by knowing your net worth. Multiple levels of income are important for financial success, so decide which ones will work best for you and get going. Remember to protect the investments you already have and know your attitude to risk before you invest. Building financial success is great fun and I love thinking of ways to increase my income and maintain my work–life balance, and I am sure you will too.

Success Box

1. Know your monthly outgoings

2. Where can you make savings?

3. What is your net worth?

4. What liquid and fixed assets do you have?

5. How can you create another income stream?

Action I Will Take

Completed on:

/   /

Action I Will Take

Completed on:

/   /

Action I Will Take

Completed on:

/   /

Action I Will Take

Completed on:

/   /

Action I Will Take

Completed on:

/   /

Action I Will Take

Completed on:

/   /

Chapter Seven

Relationship Success

You will have many relationships in your lifetime so you might as well decide now to make each of them an enjoyable experience for all concerned.

Synopsis

It is easier to change your attitude than that of another. Even a brief and transient relationship is important as it can lead to a longer and better involvement. A relationship that has broken can be repaired with patience and understanding from all parties, but this repair begins with you. This chapter offers some valuable suggestions as a basis for your relationship repair kit.

Susan Smith was a pretty baby who became an attractive child and a beautiful teenager. She had a large circle of friends of both genders. By her mid-twenties she was aware that most of her boyfriends fell short of her high expectations. Her girlfriends had now married and were raising families, and Susan was 'always the bridesmaid and never the bride'.

She pursued a successful career and acquired her own house. Soon she decided that her 'Mr Right' probably didn't exist and anyway, as an independent female she would remain single and a free spirit.

Then at a business meeting she met Paul, a junior executive from a large company. She had always been very careful about her more intimate relationships, but this was passion at first sight—her own expensive hotel room was not used that night. The passion grew into mutual love and they were married on her twenty-ninth birthday. Within the next four years they became parents to three delightful children. Susan was happy to surrender her career to become a full time wife and mother.

Paul's career progression was stratospheric and he was clearly destined for a top board position before he was 40. He was working longer and longer hours and then, when he did return home, later than ever, it was to find that his once beloved 'yummy mummy' had not even bothered to dress or apply make-up. As the standards of housekeeping visibly deteriorated he hired domestic help. To assist Susan with the children he recruited an au pair. There was not a lot he could do about her steadily increasing weight and he dismissed it as a price that had to be paid for having three children.

Soon he stopped inviting his colleagues and their spouses to lunches and dinner parties at home because, although he would never admit it to his wife, he was ashamed of the way that she had let herself go. As Paul continued his high-flying career, Susan sank deeper into a despair of domestic trivia and boredom. The gulf between them grew ever wider.

Paul's accident was his wake up call. The car was a write-off and he was lucky that he only needed minor surgery. Even so, as he stared at the walls in the post-operative recovery ward, he realised that he had allowed his priorities to skew off course. For Susan's fortieth birthday in a few days' time, he made a decision to take her back to their honeymoon hotel in Rome, leaving the children in the capable hands of her parents. She was shocked when, on their first night away, he revealed that he had been doing the sums and was going to quit his job. He would work from home and she would be involved in the business too.

The next ten days seemed to pass in a flash as they made their plans—the first time they had done anything together for far too long. They negotiated exclusive UK distribution rights to a range of Italian children's wear which they would sell via mail order. That was several years ago and now their relationship, based on shared interests and responsibilities, is stronger than it has ever been. Susan again takes a pride in her appearance. The children enjoy having a full time dad again. Even Susan's parents, flattered by having that vacation responsibility for the children, are now enjoying closer involvement with the young family.

Paul admits that his car crash was the turning point: 'I may have lost the company car in more ways than one, but I rescued all those loving relationships that are beyond any price.'

A relationship exists whenever two or more people interact. Given the population of the planet it seems inevitable that, unless we live in a remote tribe or a closed community, we will all have hundreds of such interactions every year. That is why relationship success matters. Achieve success in this and your life will progress as if it is a train on well oiled wheels. If a relationship is not developed those wheels can fall off, leading to discontent and frustration for all concerned.

SELF DIAGNOSTIC BOX

Am I good at building and maintaining relationships?

A truly successful relationship, however, exists whenever two or more people interact and when all parties are completely satisfied with the outcomes because they have received the reactions and results that they expected when the encounter started.

We learn our relationship etiquette largely by trial and error. We discover what works and do more of it. We discover what doesn't work and avoid it. Our childhood experiences and the examples of others also colour our approach to relationships.

Already it is apparent that relationship issues can cover a vast spectrum and every encounter is a unique experience, whether it is good or bad, for the parties involved. To offer you some meaningful insights, it is necessary to 'chunk down' the subject into manageable bite sizes.

Before we do that, however, I want to emphasise a basic and fundamental rule of success which states that: 'It is easier to change your own attitude than it is to attempt to change other people.' If you attempt to change some individuals, you will fail and your relationship will be damaged as a result.

Returning to our 'chunking down' idea, the first and most obvious division is to consider relationships as transient, short term, medium term and long term. It is worth remembering that every relationship begins at the transient level. Just like seeds that are planted in a garden, some will wither right there whilst others may develop and bloom as they move through the intermediate stages to become well established and long living sources of pleasure. Apart from the briefest of transient examples, every relationship has the capability to develop a life and momentum of its own and it will change and evolve with time. This means that your behaviour, even if it worked well at an early stage, will also need to change and evolve to keep your relationships successful.

The table below identifies some examples of the people with whom you may have relationships. I have also gone out on a limb to suggest some durations to further chunk them down. With this example, you should consider instances from your own life experience as you read the list.

	Minimal duration	Medium duration	Longer duration
Transient	Shop assistants	New acquaintances	Long haul flight staff
Short term	Course tutors	Repeat clients	Friendships
Mid-term	Childhood friends	Work colleagues	Employer
Long term	None	Lovers	Spouses/ partners

This is a good place to introduce another variety of relationship where the normal rules of success may not apply, simply because there is an inequality between the parties involved.

These relationships include typical 'master/slave' situations where one individual has a hold over the other as a result of rank or position. Think of relationships between teacher and pupil, warder and inmate, officers and crew, policeman and suspect, and so on. Even in these initially unpromising relationships it is possible to achieve success although the approach needed is different from more social and sociable encounters.

You will soon become a very frustrated subordinate in one of these unequal relationships if you even think of attempting to redress the balance of power. Your approach to success is to clearly and privately determine the parameters of conduct available to the other party in the areas where they have absolute control.

SELF DIAGNOSTIC BOX

How did I resolve my last unequal relationship issue?

Here you have only two courses of action—you can say 'yes' and keep them happy or you can say 'no' and put up with the consequences. You can identify areas where their authority is borderline and where you might have some limited influence in the relationship. Some 'masters' (especially those who are insecure in their position) may even seek to impose an authority in areas of the relationship where they should have none. Whether you are the 'master' or 'slave' in such relationships, the key to success is to know the true parameters of responsibility for each party and to operate within these firm boundaries.

Unless you are serving a long prison sentence, such relationships are usually temporary for the slave who can survive by putting up with it for as long as it takes and with the least conflict or hassle. As a master, be sure to conduct yourself fairly and within the rules that your position requires and where your actions are appropriate to each circumstance as it arises.

While we are looking at unequal relationships, it is worth looking at the issue of bullying. Here, one or more parties attempt to exercise control over their victim through a regime of fear or force even though they have no right whatsoever to do so. Alas, some bullies seem attracted to occupations where they can sustain a master/slave scenario. As a rule of thumb, avoiding them is usually a good way to finding peace and success.

In a bullying situation, there is always a victim and yet, conversely, there is no victor. Most of us encounter bullies. Of these bullies some go on to perpetuate their unacceptable behaviour into adulthood as abusive employers or spouses. The psychology of bullying tendencies is extremely complex but, in my opinion, they generally indicate a weakness and inadequacy on the part of the bullies. Depending on the risks and specific circumstances involved, one way to overcome a bully can be to stand up to them. Most of them will then turn their attentions elsewhere but this option is not always possible or advisable. Here is a technique I learnt over 15 years ago and it was taught to me as the acronym **DEAP**.

Describe the situation, what is happening, how it happens, the exact times it happens etc.

Explain how this makes you feel—without emotions, just as a report—read it if you need to

Assert what you want to happen instead, what needs to change in the way of behaviour/actions

Penalties or consequences should the changes not take place— you need to be able to implement them

The key to this technique being successful, especially in an emotionally charged situation such as bullying at work, is to remove the emotional responses the other person evokes in you. You do this by using the anchoring techniques described in Chapter Four to anchor a confident resourceful state. Before you arrange the meeting, make sure you have done the following:

1. Written out each part of the DEAP technique as you experienced it.
2. Put it aside for 24 hours.
3. Read what you have written, taking out all emotionally charged words and replacing them with descriptive words where possible.
4. Asked a neutral, trustworthy and well-respected person to read the text and critique.

5. Once you are satisfied your DEAP document is sound and emotion free—rehearse, rehearse, rehearse. It is the rehearsal that will make the difference. If you can say the words eloquently without emotion and despite constant interruption you will be in a position of power and it will be more probable that you will achieve the outcome you are looking for. Have printed versions in the event you might need them. Always have one printed copy as a back-up for you to read should your nerves overcome you.
6. When you are fully rehearsed arrange a meeting. Better still, get your Human Resources department to arrange a meeting with the other person where both of you can take along a silent witness.

Be brave. It is always better to take action as it puts you back in a position of equal instead of victim.

If you are being bullied you must take action by reporting it as soon as possible to the appropriate superior or to one of the many support organisations that now exist. If this fails to deliver a satisfactory outcome, then consider whether you could remove yourself from the relationship totally by changing your employment—after letting your current employer know exactly why you want to leave.

If you are in an abusive or bullying personal relationship, then seriously consider your options, and the benefits and losses of leaving it.

After that look at the dark side of relationships, let's become positive by considering the types of relationship that are more equal and where you have some freedom of action. Again, we can subdivide these relationships for clarity by considering them as casual, work related and domestic.

Casual relationships

Most casual relationships fall into the 'transient' description of the earlier chart. You will generally be in total control of these. Accept that the other party will have certain duties to perform as

their side of the bargain and that, by and large, they will undertake these to the best of their abilities. Begin every encounter with
an expectation of mutually agreeable and satisfying outcomes.
Adopt a pleasant expression and non-threatening body language.
Communicate clearly and politely and treat the other party as you
would wish to be treated if the roles were reversed. Remember the
happy difference that can be created by a smile, by 'please' and by
'thank you'.

If an encounter seems to be going off the rails, before you ask the other person for help, get very clear on your out-come—what do you want to happen? Most humans are happy to help so, even if you have a complaint, instead of storming in with all guns blaz-ing, begin with, 'I need your help because ...' Quietly and briefly explain the issue as you see it and immediately shut up to allow the other person to consider and suggest the pos-sible options. The words 'help' and 'because' are immensely powerful in defusing a poten-

SELF DIAGNOSTIC BOX

How do I respond when I am asked for help and the word 'because' is included?

tially explosive encounter (see Chapter Nine, Influencing Success).
If the person on the receiving end of your complaint is unable
to deal with it to your satisfaction, then seek a discussion with
their supervisor, manager or whoever is next up in the chain of
responsibility.

Low 'n' slow

This is a great tip that I use when confronted with difficult situations. It is the simplest technique you will learn in this book and
yet it is one of the most powerful ones. All you need to do is to
speak in a very low tone and at a slower pace.

If you lower your tone by one or two levels you will defuse the situation. Determine your normal level of speaking and mark the level out of 10, where 10 is shouting and 0 is not speaking, and practise going up and down the scale until you know what number you speak at normally. Now all you do is lower your voice one or two levels. For example, if you find your normal voice tone is level 6 on your scale then during confrontation or conflict, lower your tone by two levels. Use the same technique for your speed of speaking, with level 10 being so fast it is nearly garbled and 0 is not speaking.

Practice your low 'n' slow often so that when you really need to call upon the skill you can do so quickly and easily without causing any offence. It should be seamless as you drop from normal to the lower level and slower speed. The change in tone and speed works in two areas: one, it gives your subconscious a signal that you are in control and there is no need to panic (no need to release the adrenalin into your system) and, two, it signals to other people that you are not going to be confrontational and yet you are also strongly in control.

Usually, when we are afraid, angry, incensed, enraged, cross, furious or feeling any other passionate negative emotional response our voice announces this to the world. Your voice can become high and squeaky, loud and caustic or any variation other than your normal voice, and by controlling your response to low 'n' slow you control the situation and do not reveal your emotionally weakened position. It gives you flexibility and time to think things through and also it can disperse that very negative 'butterflies in the stomach' response.

By following these tips you will more often than not gain the outcomes that you desire. If you have a volatile personality, please do whatever it takes to keep your temper under control because you lose respect and negotiating options along with your temper. Learn the anchoring technique in Chapter Five, Self Success, to gain confidence, calmness and control. A loss of temper reflects badly on your own maturity and emotional stability and could make the other person more determined not to help you! Avoid making a threat in the heat of the moment and, if you feel that threats are the only recourse open to you (they rarely are), then never threaten an action that you are not willing and able to follow through. When you stay cool, calm and collected you retain the upper hand and at the same time keep all your options open.

Work-related relationships

Work depends on good relationships whatever your job, career, vocation or employment. Even if you are a 'one-man band' working from home, you will have relationships with your clients and with the various regulatory authorities who have hoops that must be jumped through under pain of legal penalties.

In any work environment, you will have relationships with superiors, subordinates and peers. If you are a managing director or chief executive it may seem that you have no superiors. However, they are just disguised as stakeholders, shareholders, bankers, the government and local authorities, as these are all entities which can either restrict or facilitate your freedom of action.

As the boss, your success at building good relationships can have a significant impact on the entire venture or business. In extreme cases it may even give you a competitive edge when it comes to recruitment, retention of staff, the acquisition of new customers or negotiating favourable terms with suppliers. It is sometimes said that a chain is only as strong as its weakest link and in the corporate world your success is only as strong as your weakest relationship.

If you are a team leader, supervisor, manager, foreman or have any responsibility for others, then your relationship with these subordinates will determine your own success and progress. The key word here is 'rapport' (see Chapter Ten, Neuro-Linguistic Programming Success) where your main outcome is to share your own objectives and aims with those below you. This will allow them to see where you are heading and why you ask them to perform certain duties.

Your key quality must be fairness. This means that you treat everyone alike and do not play any games of favourites or victims. You need the respect of your subordinates and this will be earned by example and experience. If you demand respect you will not achieve it; instead you will receive a thin veneer of apparent respect which can conceal a nest of fermenting resentment and bloody-mindedness.

Your peers may be equal in the words of your employment contracts and wages; however, they will never be equal when it comes to personalities, skills, talents, experience, abilities, emotions and any of the other complexities that make us individuals. Here, relationship success is probably best described as harmony and balance. In any group there will be hidden agendas and vested interests which can colour the conduct of your encounters.

Some people may be industrious and efficient whilst others may adopt a far more relaxed attitude to work. You will not get on with everyone to the same extent as you will naturally like some people more than others. Endeavour to just accept them all as they are, without judgement or criticism. Another word for peers is equal, so if it is not your job to motivate or change them, it is quite alright not to have an opinion or to keep your opinions to yourself.

Be even handed, avoid gossip and never say anything about anyone that would embarrass either of you if the other party overheard your comments. I was taught at a very young age, 'If you cannot say something good about someone, it is better to say nothing at all.'

When you have relationships with subordinates, the rules change slightly because you have an implicit edge to sustain and maintain. This is not usually a problem because most organisations have a hierarchy of rules, protocols, procedures and 'custom and practice' that are understood by all and which offer basic guidelines concerning conduct.

Even if it is not laid down, you have a duty of care to your subordinates, especially when they have personal problems that can have an adverse impact on their productivity and accuracy. Your own future will depend to some extent on the results that they achieve. Without interference you can help them to deliver at the peak of their abilities. Respect any confidences that are shared with you. Be firm and fair, avoid taking sides and never, ever, abuse your position of power or authority.

If you have any strong feelings about race, gender, ethnicity, age or cultures just leave them at home and keep them to yourself. These are your personal demons or hang-ups so don't share them with anyone else. You may like to take a few moments of introspection about any such attitudes that you harbour and ask yourself if they still serve you well. Such feelings and attitudes are invariably negative and limiting, so although it may take some time, just let them go to the best of your abilities.

SELF DIAGNOSTIC BOX

Am I willing to control my prejudices, if doing so will improve my relationships?

Transactional analysis

Transactional analysis (TA) was developed by psychiatrist Eric Berne during the 1950s. It is not my intention to go into great depth in this chapter, only to give you an overview that will enable you to understand how you are interacting with others and hopefully give you the inspiration to research TA in more depth based on your own experiences. According to TA there are three main 'ego states' through which we communicate—the Parent ego, the Adult ego and the Child ego—and it is how these ego states interact that forms the basis of transactional analysis. I will briefly explain the ego states with the possible behaviors we demonstrate when we are in them and how to get the best from our communications with this information. The first thing I want to point out is that an ego state, like any emotional state, is transient and you will experience many ego states in one day.

The three main states

The Parent ego state is divided into two distinct behavioural responses: the Nurturing Parent and the Critical Parent.

The Child ego state is known as the 'feeling' state and is divided into two distinct behavioral responses: the Adaptive Child and the Free Child.

The Adult ego state is the 'thought' state and does not have any divisions.

Before we look at how this information is of use to you, it is important to provide a brief overview of the behaviours related to each ego state. This will make it easier for you to identify when you are in each ego state and therefore what responses you can expect from other people around you. Overleaf, have a look at the positive side of each ego state in Table A and the negative impacts in Table B and then reflect on the times you may have been reacting from each of the ego states.

How can you use this information? Well, once you can identify when you are reacting from each individual ego state you will begin to recognise the ego states of the people around you and finally you will be able to influence the situation. Transactional analysis looks at the way communication take place between humans involving, 'I do something to you, and you do something back.' Berne's theory is that effective transactions (communications) must be complementary. This means that two people must be in the same ego state for both individuals to be easily understood and for the communication to be effective, Parent to Parent, Adult to Adult and Child to Child where both people involved are in the same ego state and communicating easily.

Think about the last time you communicated with your best friend. What ego states were you both communicating from? Were you both in a Free Child ego state, having a giggle about something that happened or were you both in Critical Parent ego states discussing the vagaries of the youth today? Either way, you will probably discover that you were both in the same ego state and therefore communicating effectively and feeling comfortable.

Problems, anger, arguments and frustration occur during communications when the transactions between two people become crossed; when one person is in a different ego state to the other person. If a manager is in an Adult ego state as he enters the office to

Table A – Positive effect

Nurturing parent	Setting boundaries, upholding the rules, law abiding, advising, traditional, value driven	Critical parent
Adult	Information gathering, alternative seeking, organising, planning, problem solving, probability analysis, contemplative, evaluating	
Adaptive child	Mannerly, courteous, rule abiding, apologetic, appropriate behaviour, asks for help, submissive	Free child	Loves, laughs, has fun, adventurous, trusting, creative, intuitive, curious

Table B – Negative effect

Nurturing parent	Smothering, over-protective, restricting growth, suppressing, suffocating, restraining	Critical parent	Disciplining, judging, critical, domineering, bullying, harassing, doctrine driven, dictating
Adult	Boring, dull, tedious, dreary, analysis paralysis, unemotional evaluating, emotionally distant, droll, Mr Spock (from *Star Trek*) characteristics		
Adaptive child	Continuous apologising, whining, sighing, withdrawn, guilt ridden, resentful, bitter, victim, pained	Free child	Manipulative, hates, vindictive, mean, nasty, cruel, bullying, spiteful, malicious, horrible, malevolent

find a group of employees throwing paper planes around the room and laughing (Free Child ego state), this could (and frequently does) push the manager into Critical Parent ego state, and he raises his voice and orders them to get back to work. The employees will respond in either Free Child saying under their breath, 'Stupid git, just cos' he's not having fun!' or the Adaptive Child thinking, 'Oh my! Now I am for it!' The interesting thing about ego states is that once you are in an ego state you can perpetuate the crossed transactions indefinitely. This means that if your boss is in Critical Parent ego state you will respond in your preferred Child ego state and if you respond in your Child ego state it will force your boss to respond in the Parent ego state. Round and round you will both go, feeling the other person does not understand you.

A guiding principle for smoothing tense relationships is to recognise the ego state you are communicating from and the ego state your recipient is communicating from and find a complementary state for both of you. This means that you both use the same ego state and therefore can 'speak in the same language'. An effective way of dealing with difficult communications is to initially join the other person in their ego state (complementary communication) and communicate in the same ego state for a short period. Once rapport has been established in that ego state you can lead him/her into another more productive ego state according to your desired outcome. This process is known as 'pace, pace, lead'. You join him/her, match their communicating behaviour for a while (pace, pace) then move to the ego state better suited to the transaction, leading the other person with you. You must be fully in rapport to do this successfully.

Transactional analysis is a massive topic and, as I stated, it is my intention to inspire curiosity in the subject so you undertake further research and learn the intricacies of this fascinating communicating approach, as I am sure you will find it invaluable for successful relationship building.

Domestic relationships

In many ways, what goes on in your household is a mirror image of the work situation. Parents are the equivalent to the director or CEO, siblings of a similar age are like a peer group and any younger members of the home could be seen as subordinates. Read the previous section again and see how it might correspond to your own domestic arrangements.

Despite the impression given by the media, especially the red top tabloids and the more lurid Sunday newspapers, most families are not dysfunctional and work their way through temporary crises without undue drama.

Until the mid-1950s in Britain (earlier in the US), it was generally accepted that marriage was for life and divorce was rare. In the twenty-first century, cohabitation accounts for a significant percentage of all domestic relationships with, according to a recent report, as many as half of all children being 'born out of wedlock'. So what changed? It would appear that a national awareness grew that it was probably unreasonable to expect a relationship of marital harmony to last for a lifetime. This is a valid outlook but what it leads to may be deeply flawed. In the old days, couples would work through their differences and difficulties and in doing so would learn the intricate skills of communication and relationship building. They may also have experienced humility and the complexity of compromise. The current approach seems to reflect our consumer society where, if something is broken, it is easier to replace it than to repair it.

The key to successful domestic relationships can be described in two words—communication and respect. Winston Churchill had it right when he stated, 'jaw-jaw is better than war-war'. If you are aware of deteriorating relationships with a spouse, partner, children or relatives, first identify why you think there is deterioration. Be aware that it may only exist in your imagination

> **SELF DIAGNOSTIC BOX**
>
> Have I explored every possibility to repair a relationship instead of ending it?

or your misinterpretation of the facts. If there really is a problem, then as unemotionally as you can, distil it down to a basic and simple statement based on the facts. Write this down.

Next, write down the ideal resolution that could repair the situation from your own point of view. Now repeat the process as the other person, as if you were in their shoes. Consider and write down how you believe those actions would affect the other party or parties involved. If there is a gulf between these two statements, then see if you can modify your own 'best outcome' so that it can build a bridge between you. Once you have defined the best win-win outcomes, determine what actions you can take to begin the healing process. Then apply them. It is said that pride comes before a fall—know that it will also never heal your relationships.

Previously sound relationships do not go bad overnight. There is a gradual erosion of trust, love, respect or harmony. There will be disappointments and differences of opinion and these inflict wounds that will take time to heal. Allow as much time as necessary to first stop any further deterioration and then to begin the repair. Your relationship may have started when you listened to your heart; it will be repaired when you use your head. Avoid making accusations or bringing up past issues in the heat of the moment and never, ever resort to violence, either physical or verbal.

There is another element that is of almost equal importance and that can be even more difficult to apply. It is forgiveness. To conclude this chapter I leave you with a couple of thoughts to ponder on as they affect your life. If you become a human doormat, don't be surprised if people walk all over your relationships. Second, there are some relationships that are truly beyond rescue and here, when you have explored all the possible considerations of communication, counselling, coaching and conciliation, you may be left with only one option—to terminate the relationship. Make no mistake; this can be an easy option to choose and a difficult one to apply.

I have concentrated on difficult relationships during this chapter as I believe that if you already have good relationships and know how to deal with difficult situations you are ahead of the game. I found training to become a master practitioner in Neuro-Linguistic

Programming a great ameliorative for my communication skills and highly recommend the study of this fascinating topic.

Success Box

1. Identify one area where you feel that you do not enjoy a successful relationship

2. Without emotion and with focus on the true facts, write down the issue in a few simple words

3. Consider and write the best possible outcome from your point of view and define actions that you could take to realise it

4. Now consider that outcome from the other person's viewpoint to see if it is likely to be acceptable to them

5. Using the answers to 3 and 4 above, seek a win–win situation. Define this with the next action needed to make it happen

6. Implement it as soon as possible

Action I Will Take
Completed on:
/ /

Action I Will Take
Completed on:
/ /

Action I Will Take
Completed on:
/ /

Action I Will Take
Completed on:
/ /

Action I Will Take
Completed on:
/ /

Action I Will Take
Completed on:
/ /

Chapter Eight

Spiritual Success

Find space, peace and tranquillity to enhance your successes in all other areas of your life.

Synopsis

You will discover what spirituality means to you and others. You will journey into your purpose and see how many routes there can be towards spiritual success.

Robert Byron and his wife Cynthia are thoroughly enjoying their retirement. They are both 70 and are more active and alert than some people half their age. It hardly seems possible to either of them when they recall that Robert's fiftieth birthday was almost his last. His doctor said he was a heart attack looking for somewhere to happen.

Robert had worked for the National Health Service since leaving school. He was a conscientious soul who worked his way up the career ladder until he became responsible for sourcing and negotiating supply prices and deliveries for a dozen major hospitals and a hundred health clinics. That was when his stress levels reached breaking point and he consulted his doctor, who prescribed drugs.

In less than a year he became an irascible and unpleasant person. At work, his staff now dreaded having to talk to him and sought transfers to other departments. At home, Cynthia now admits that she even considered moving out because he was such a misery and their grown-up children, who were previously regular visitors at the family home, found excuses not to call. Robert even disliked himself and knew that his behaviour was unfair, untypical and irrational.

A medical representative, who always took Robert out for lunch when they had completed their business, left a book behind in the office. Robert was about to sling it in the bin when he noticed the back cover blurb. It said, in big bold lettering, 'Explore the Mind, Body, Spirit Connection'. He shut his office door and read the book from cover to cover that afternoon. Although it is now dog-eared and well worn he keeps it as a reminder of the day his life changed.

The chapter on meditation seemed to talk to him personally. It explained the importance of controlled relaxation, made some amazing claims for the benefits that could arise from following a simple daily routine and offered case histories exploring the connection between physical health and spiritual peace.

Instead of sitting in his office working through lunch time, Robert started taking a daily stroll around the park beside the hospital, invariably stopping for 15 minutes of relaxation at a bench that was almost hidden in the trees. Within a few weeks he became aware of the birds, insects and small animals that inhabited the undergrowth and trees. He noticed clouds and the almost daily growth of some of the plants and shrubs.

To his amazement, his stress seemed to melt away and he was able to do his work tasks with an ease that he had long forgotten. Eventually, Cynthia could no longer contain her curiosity about the beneficial changes that she noticed. She said, 'I got my Robert back.' As a very pragmatic and practical man he found it difficult to explain his new 'discoveries' to her. He said, 'I obviously know about the mind and body connection, but that whole spirit thing was hard for me to swallow. I suppose I realised that I had nothing to lose by giving it a try.'

This chapter is about you discovering what spirituality means to you and how you define it. Before you can proceed, please do not confuse spirituality with religion. Many people who are happy with their spirituality have no religion at all and many others, who follow a religion, can struggle with their spirituality. You can also discover your life purpose if you have not already done this and explore many different ideas about spirituality.

Before you read this chapter you need to discover what it means to you right now; then you will be able to measure your progress.

Answer these questions:

1. What do I think of when I consider the word 'spirituality'?
2. What does being spiritual mean to me?
3. How do I know this?
4. Define spiritually as it is for you.

There are many different interpretations of spirituality. Unlike material, worldly or earthly where most objects are tangible and visible, spirituality is invisible and powerful and is a totally personal experience.

SELF DIAGNOSTIC BOX

How do I define spirituality?

Here I invite you to consider spirituality as a connection to something 'greater' than yourself. This may include an emotional state or a religious reverence. It can relate to psychological health and it often focuses on personal experience, as it does in some religions.

Spirituality can involve perceiving life as having more important, more integrated or more complex dimensions than the usual 'busyness' of the daily business. You will come across terms like 'higher being' or 'enlightened state' especially as contrasted with the merely sensual, physical state.

You have spiritual success when you achieve inner peace.

Humans have sought inner peace since before recorded history and, just as today when a need is perceived, there were people willing to share their own experiences, to teach others and to guide them along the paths to spirituality that worked for them. Soon there were followers of some of these guides who then developed an entire protocol of procedures. There are thousands of such guides and you will surely be familiar with the names of at least a few: mystics, Zen masters, Sufis, yogis, shamans, imams, rabbi, priests and monks. They all attract followers but you do not need to be a follower to be spiritual as it is perfectly normal to find your own path of discovery. However, if you are involved with any religion that provides you with spiritual insights and comfort, then stay with it as you consider the broader views of this chapter.

General spirituality

There are many different interpretations of what is, or is not, spirituality and here I will have a look at a few to give you some options to consider on your journey.

Religion is the most obvious form of spirituality. There are many religions in the world, each with different rules and regulations and most of them are based on the follower having faith in an external force. Your religious preferences will largely depend on where you were born, family influences and your exposure to different denominations. Your religion will have shaped your beliefs and spiritual growth to this point. I am not advocating religion nor am I denigrating religion. It is a form of spirituality for some people.

Here it is worth mentioning that a belief in some external force, often described as universal, eternal and ubiquitous, is not an excuse to waive your rights of free choice to make things happen in your life. You are, and remain, in personal control of your own destiny. Faith in a higher intelligence can be a great help when the going gets tough.

Giving to receive

For some people, the pure act of giving or contributing is in itself a spiritual experience which represents all the spiritual success or satisfaction they need. In many faiths and cultures over the years, the practice of tithing has offered a route into this spiritual state. Generally, the tithing or regular giving of ten per cent of your income towards the support of a spiritual organisation or spiritual leaders is the normal practice.

> **SELF DIAGNOSTIC BOX**
>
> How do I contribute to society?

If this giving is done from the heart with happiness and joy, the giver usually experiences a spiritual lift and even praise for their contribution. Sadly, tithing can also become a duty or a burden and the spiritually lifting experience is lost with its associated commitment.

Contribution to charities in the form of a regular donation can be a spiritual experience. If you really want to experience the spirituality of giving, then give of your time as a volunteer because in these hectic days we are always short of time. If time is a precious commodity for you it follows that giving it to someone else is the greater gift. Also, when you are interacting with other people by providing a needed service to the betterment of others, you will always gain from the experience in one way or another.

There are many opportunities to give of your time as a volunteer. Consider what is important to you (look at Chapter Five, Self Success), what you value and then match that to a charity needing volunteers. Usually, you will be asked to undertake some training before you can assist and this is a great way to meet people who share your values and to learn new skills—all this before you have even contributed! This is a win–win scenario.

Philanthropic actions fall into the category of contribution. If you look at any list of the world's richest people you will discover that many of them have created financial trust funds that enable them to share their fortunes. If these arrangements are made for tax avoidance purposes or publicity, there will be limited correspond ing spiritual gain. There may even be a loss or erosion of that individual's spirituality.

Here are a few guidelines for giving as a path to spirituality.

* Give time or money freely within what you can afford after compliance with your legal and personal obligations
* Give to the source or cause that you can identify with as having helped you spiritually
* Give with no expectation of material gain, personal publicity or other reward
* Give because you want to and not because you have to

Look for the joy, growth and learning that can come from giving and you will always find it.

Peace and meditation

The search for spiritual peace often leads to people learning meditation techniques. Many of these are included as parts of religious observance, but simple meditation techniques are available to anyone. They are a means of disconnecting from the hustle and bustle of this modern world. Regularly take a few minutes out each day to relax in stillness as you take a break from your search for material gains and emotional highs.

If you do not know how to be still in mind and body, your energies are being used up and not replenished. It is sometimes claimed, by those who practise meditation, that a single 20-minute session can be as refreshing as an hour of sleep. Simple meditation allows you to achieve inner stillness. You can discover that it will lead to insights, inspiration, spiritual awareness and even the answers to questions that have eluded you.

Deepak Chopra is a popular author on spiritual matters and, in his book *The Seven Spiritual Laws of Success*, he has given the reader seven separate guidance chapters. He states that we have pure potentiality which can be reached through taking time to be silent.

The art of journaling

If you are not yet ready to explore meditation, you may find that journaling offers you a more practical or prosaic way of getting in touch with your spirituality. Journaling has been popular in the US for many years and yet it seems to have a limited appeal in Britain which is a pity, because it can be a powerful and helpful tool.

Your journal has very similar geography to a diary; whereas your diary is used for appointments and reminders or even factual accounts of what has just happened, your journal opens up options of creative freedom. Put very simply, your journal is a secret record where you write about your thoughts, ideas, dreams, goals, insights, annoyances, happiness and insights arising from the upsides and downsides of your life. The physical act of writing creates a mental path of release and stillness. The main rule is that you should write as fast as you can without editing your thoughts as you go; just write down whatever comes to mind. With practise you will soon find that your thoughts and words can take you in unexpected directions. When, from time to time, you choose to read your journal, you may well detect cycles of mood and emotion; you will discover that some material matters that seemed important at the time have now assumed trivial dimensions.

SELF DIAGNOSTIC BOX
When was the last time I regularly meditated or wrote a journal?

There is a very useful tip concerning both meditation and journaling and it is to do with the way that humans can adopt new habits. When you do the same thing, at the same time, in the same place and in the same way each day, you will find that within a week, that routine will become a habit which is hard to break. You will feel that there is something missing if you don't do it. You will become even more spiritually empowered if you create your own little ritual around these activities, like preparing your chair or desk or taking several deep breaths before you begin a session. In this context, ritual does not mean dressing up in fancy kaftans or adopting strange body positions, although there is no reason why you should not do this if you wish and find that it helps!

Some people meditate and journal in silence, others prefer to play some appropriate music to set the mood and to mask out traffic sounds or other distractions. I know one person who always plays Bach or Mozart at low levels at such times, and another prefers to play 'ambient recordings' or Gregorian Chants (which are, in themselves, prayerful meditations). Remembering that your objective is calm, peace and stillness, it is highly improbable that the latest flavour of pop music will help you to achieve these relaxing and restorative spiritual states.

Inner peace

Inner peace differs from the state of being peaceful for meditation. Inner peace is unique to each of us and therefore I can only *suggest* what it might be like for you.

You could experience a sense or a feeling of being held gently in the arms of love, peace, harmony and joy. You may have a sensation of light-ness and confidence in the assured knowing that there is an inexhaust-ible supply of unshakeable inner resources to smooth your passage through any situation. Regardless of life's challenges you do have the ability to think of a solution and to easily overcome problems by imple-menting it.

When you achieve inner peace you have calmness, serenity and a relaxed manner because you know the universe is abundant and will

SELF DIAGNOSTIC BOX

Can I reach inner peace no matter what is happening around me?

provide for you without your striving or straining for anything. Life is full of a rich abundance which manifests itself in any form you need, exactly when you need it. Truly knowing this at your core being is one of the definitions of inner peace.

Enlightenment

What is enlightenment and is it spiritual? Buddhism has ten life states, the highest of which is Buddhahood—the state of enlighten-ment. When you achieve this level of enlightenment you become a sentient being with fully developed positive qualities and no negative qualities.

In Zen, enlightenment is the state of being with no mind and no ego. It is freedom from beliefs, opinions, ideals and concepts through a lack of identification with the body and the mind.

Some people define enlightenment as 'brightening', which roughly means the achievement of a new wisdom or a new understanding which enables clarity of awareness. In English, there are two common conceptual definitions, which are poles apart, so take care not to confuse them: distinct religious or spiritual enlightenment and intellectual enlightenment.

Enlightenment is frequently associated with a religious experience which can become almost euphoric. Intellectual enlightenment is often linked to the intellectual movement known as the Age of Enlightenment or the Age of Reason.

What really matters to you, when considering enlightenment in a context of spiritual success, is what it means to you and if you ever feel you have reached it. The final all powerful question is, can you replicate it when you need or want to?

Euphoric state

Is this what you seek more than the other areas? Personal honesty is required for you to determine what drives you to search for fulfilment and the means by which you get it. The pursuit of pleasure does not have to mean a materialistic reward. It can be as simple as the great glow of satisfaction you experience when you know that you have done something extremely well. In Chapter Five, I explained that Abraham Maslow wrote a paper titled *A Theory of Human Motivation* in which he hypothesised about a hierarchy of needs where self-actualisation is the highest need—that is to be the best we can be, which can translate into spiritual awareness.

There are many different ways of reaching euphoria, a state where every fibre of your being is in heightened awareness of the moment to the exclusion of all other stimuli. Some people achieve it temporarily in sexual intercourse, others in extreme sports participation or the mass hysteria of a public event. There are natural links between the many sources of euphoric experience in that they are not pharmaceutical.

Euphoria can be triggered from the release of endorphins into the blood stream. Endorphins are produced by the pituitary gland and the hypothalamus as a reaction to block pain, and at the same time create a feeling of well-being (it is said that they act in the same way as opiates). This release also happens when you take part in strenuous physical exercise.

Marathon runners mention a state called 'The Wall', which is where they are near exhaustion and in pain, feeling they cannot go on, whilst at the same time continuing to run. They feel a sudden rush of euphoria overcoming those body signals and this enables them to continue. Many runners are addicted to 'The Wall' effect and push themselves ever harder even through injury.

It also explains how individuals can become addicted to sexual intercourse and lose normal moral guidelines in order to satisfy the need for the euphoric experience. How does this happen? Your brain consists of neurons and receptors. Endorphins attach themselves to these 'receptors' acting like a chemical plug fitting into the neuron socket.

Now you do not need to take part in strenuous exercise or throw yourself into the next available orgy to self-induce euphoria. You can use the anchoring technique, explained in Chapter Four, Emotional Success, and simply anchor a powerful euphoric experience or memory, releasing the anchor when you need to.

Spiritual success is not about striving for a state of permanent euphoria. Any attempts to sustain this enjoyable high for too long, or too often, will lead at best to disappointment and at worst, to mental or physical breakdown. Euphoria is like the powerful reheat afterburner function that enables a jet engine aircraft to boost its way out of danger. It is like the brilliance of a photoflood light bulb that will burn brightly but briefly compared with the life of its domestic counterpart. Euphoria can be reached at any time you need to call upon it once you have perfected the art of its recall.

Part of the natural world

Communing with nature is also a way of tapping into a feeling of spiritual well-being. When you go into a beautiful forest, when you walk along the shoreline, when you lie down in the long grass on a warm summer day, or enjoy a hot drink after a cold swim or snow blown walk, any of these as well as hundreds more examples, will make you feel good if you choose to let them. The choice is always yours!

This planet is a wonderful place that is designed to operate in perfect balance and perfection. Even natural phenomena, which we may term as disasters, have a purpose. Some forest plants actually need to be burnt away in a major fire as part of their reproductive cycle. Many disasters, however, are the results of human activity through the exploitation of natural resources or attempts to intervene in the natural cycle. As individuals, we may not be able to redress the balance but we can discover the miracles of nature by simply developing our awareness and powers of observation. Focus on what is right in our wonderful world and spend less time on the sensational headlines of the day. We are part of nature so take time out to reflect and reconnect with your natural roots. When was the last time that you looked at a pebble, a feather, a colourful leaf, a spider's web at dawn, the sunset at dusk? I mean really look and marvel at the wonders of nature with no attempt at analysis, judgement or anything else other than pure enjoyment.

A spokesman for London's Royal Botanic Gardens at Kew, speaking on the twentieth anniversary of the major storm that swept across Southern England in 1987 said: 'We thought we had to replant everything and advised local authorities on tree replacement policies. We would not do that now. Man will plant trees according to a tape measure but nature seeds them where they are most likely to thrive. Nature has this magnificent healing power and we learned that human intervention should be minimal.'

Pleasure triggers

Eating chocolate (or drinking hot chocolate) increases the levels of neurotransmitters, such as endorphins, serotonin and phenyl ethylamine being released into the brain and thus increasing the feeling of well-being. Serotonin is an anti-depressant. One of the chemicals found in chocolate that causes the release of serotonin is tryptophan. Phenyl ethylamine works like an amphetamine and has been called the 'love drug' because it quickens the pulse and this can feel similar to the feelings released when someone falls in love. You can certainly find instant gratification inside the wrapper of your favourite chocolate bar but this is not enlightenment—it is not spiritual and it is not a lasting pleasure.

Your question, then, is: 'What is the ultimate and lasting pleasure that I can derive from my life?'

SELF DIAGNOSTIC BOX
What are my pleasure triggers?

You can start to discover the answer when you know your purpose in life. When did you last ask yourself 'What is my purpose?' and then really look for the answer. Do you have compelling reasons for just being? You see, there is not just one finite purpose or a final 'thing to do'. Your purpose can reach far beyond that. It includes your direction, your role and your contribution aligned with your desires. You need passion which, in turn, fuels the motivation for achieving your life purpose.

Here is a simple exercise to start the journey of life purpose. Go to a private peaceful place. Sit in a comfortable position and take a few slow, deep, breaths as you focus on the air going into your lungs and leaving your lungs. Now let your mind wander freely and create an imaginary life for yourself. Spend time creating all the aspects of this other life, letting your creative mind have freedoms you would not normally afford it.

Now that you have spread your creative wings and freed yourself from life's constraints you can develop your imagery by knowing more about yourself as you are now.

1. Make a list of *all* the things you really enjoy doing.
2. Now go back and look closely at the list and highlight the things you enjoy doing which you are also uniquely good at, have an easy skill in or you excel in.
3. Repeat the imagery exercise and this time include your talents from number 2 and see what happens to your imaginary life.

Secondlife.com is full of people who have created imaginary lives for themselves and as a by-product they have found a better life journey in the real world. If you would like to do a full life purpose exercise, go to Chapter Twelve, Career Success, as there is a detailed process you can follow that could make the experience more meaningful for you.

Metaphysics

Metaphysical literature asserts that we create our own reality by our continuous thoughts. How does this work? Well, in very simplistic terms, science has proved that we are all made up of atoms of energy and that nothing is static. This includes all the objects we believe are solid like mountains, wood, brick, metals and so on.

The proponents of metaphysics believe that, because thoughts are created by energy generated and flowing from the motor neurons in our brains, it creates the reality we call our lives. The Law of Attraction states that our physical and mental experiences are manifestations that correspond directly to our predominant thoughts, words, feelings and actions. Thus they surmise that we have direct control over our own reality and our own lives through our own thoughts. Metaphysics has moved from its slightly, to some minds hippy-dippy 'New Age' origins, to become a legitimate avenue

SELF DIAGNOSTIC BOX

Is what I think about most of the time positive or negative?

of academic study. Its new horizons now include the interrelationships between health, medicine, psychology, philosophy and religion, to name just a few.

A thought attracts a corresponding positive or negative experience. This leads to the concept that 'what you think about is what you will experience', an idea that has been popular among certain philosophers and denominational devotees for centuries. There is a famous quote said to be from Gautama, also known as Sakyamuni, the key figure in Buddhism: 'What you have become is the result of what you have thought.' The followers of the Law of Attraction have used this quote as a form of proof to support the theory along with a Jewish proverb, 'As a man thinketh in his heart, so he is.' They also claim that quantum physics backs the theories.

There are five things you need to do in order to set the Law of Attraction into action:

1. Decide specifically what you want and ask the universe for it.
2. Focus your thoughts and feelings upon the thing you desire.
3. Feel and behave as if your desire has already happened.
4. Open yourself to receiving it—allow that it can happen.
5. Give thanks for all that you have.

Now if you spend time thinking of what you do not want to happen this will also manifest itself. This implies that you need to avoid 'negative' thoughts; concentrate on 'positive' thoughts and the universe will manifest your desires. According to the Law of Attraction, you do not need any further input than the steps mentioned above. It is all about faith, as are many religious beliefs.

Releasing the need for control

The general edict from organised spirituality seems to require that you relinquish your need for self-control. Within the religious context, it seems to also require that you relinquish your self-control to the power of religious leaders or guides; this turns you into a follower.

Defining what gives you the feelings of well-being, peace, love, fulfilment, enlightenment, euphoria or any of the other states aligned with spirituality, is what is really important on an individual level. It really does not matter what others say, think or believe. Spirituality seems to come down to our own interpretations of what it means to us. How can I feel connected either to the universe or to a group of believers? How can I reach a state of tranquillity? How can I find euphoria and is it the route to this state that defines my spirituality?

The starting point for spiritual success is to acknowledge that spirituality is an important part of humanity and then to see where your unique paths of discovery take you, even if this means that you walk the road less travelled and march to the beat of a different drummer. Spend time and seek your own spirituality—the time and effort will reap its own rewards.

Success Box

1. Define what spirituality means to you

2. Do some imagery to gain clarity

3. Explore different routes to spirituality

4. Make a list of the things you enjoy doing

5. Decide if you want to be a follower

Action I Will Take

Completed on:

/   /

Action I Will Take

Completed on:

/   /

Action I Will Take

Completed on:

/   /

Action I Will Take

Completed on:

/   /

Action I Will Take

Completed on:

/   /

Action I Will Take

Completed on:

/   /

Chapter Nine

Influencing Success

Influence your own success with integrity.

Synopsis

Influencing happens all the time. Either we are influencing others or we are being influenced by others. You get to choose which you will do.

It is said that opposite personalities are attracted to each other. To their friends, this seemed the only possible explanation why Arthur and Martha met, courted and eventually married. She was petite and dainty, a happy-go-lucky soul who was always willing to please. He was built like a bull with a temperament to match. As a younger man he was known to be obstinate but now, even his friends were more likely to describe his demeanour as the personification of bloody-mindedness.

This oddly matched couple seemed happy together, despite the sometimes frosty atmosphere in their home. This was evident when they were discussing their first big holiday in several years. He said, 'We are going to Hollywood. I have decided and that's that!' She said, quietly, 'I had rather hoped we could go to Australia and visit my sister.'

Martha knew, from bitter experience, that Arthur liked nothing better than a head-on clash where he could dig his heels in and behave like a dictator until, through brute force and ignorance, he got his own way. He was not the sharpest knife in the box when it came to intelligence. What Martha lacked in strength, she made up for with cunning. After all their years together she knew that her husband was one of life's 'opposers'. If someone remarked that the weather was hot, he would say that it was colder than this time last year. If a waiter brought him the rare steak that he had ordered, he would always send it back because it 'must still be running around in the blasted kitchen'.

Martha had just read a magazine article about the art of influence and persuasion. 'Yes dear,' she said, 'I'll pick up the brochures about Hollywood trips tomorrow. I will really look forward to seeing the homes of the stars and shopping on Rodeo Drive.' The next evening, Arthur was in another black mood. He swept the USA brochures aside: 'It is such a phoney place—all glitz and glitter. I wouldn't go there if they paid me.'

A little later, as they had secretly arranged, Martha's sister phoned. Martha told her husband: 'She said you wouldn't like it at all out there. The Gold Coast where she lives is just like a mini California. She thinks we would be happier down in Perth if we went to Australia at all.' The sisters laughed together a few weeks later in a beach house. They had conspired to use Arthur's attitudes to their own advantages, a strategy that worked like a dream. As Arthur strutted his ample form along the expansive beaches of the Gold Coast, he hadn't the faintest inkling that he had been influenced to such a degree.

Influence takes place all the time. You are influencing, or you are being influenced by people (alive or dead), situations, events, weather, animals, and just about anything else you can name. There is a catch in that last sentence. If you go to the trouble of naming something, you have been influenced by it.

When you are adept at influencing others you can inspire, motivate, gain support, persuade, sell, enlist champions, engage their imagination, create relationships and create a positive impact. Influence is so powerful that you really do need to know how to use it to get the results you are looking for. Successful influencing is a combination of good communication, interpersonal skills,

SELF DIAGNOSTIC BOX

What influencing skills do I already have?

146

clear presentation and assertiveness techniques. You also need to adapt the approach according to the requirements of your circumstances.

To consistently apply influence, you will need to invest time in developing these skills. A useful starting point is to gain an awareness of the effect that you currently have on other people. Once you are conscious of this, you can adapt and modify your personal style to get the outcomes that you want, whilst still being true to yourself. This requires constant slight adjustments to your behaviour and attitude whilst not changing who you are, how you feel and what you think. Influencing success is neither coercion nor manipulation; it is subtle persuasion that shifts perceptions.

Coercion and manipulation

Some people rely on overt coercion and covert manipulation to influence others. Although they might sometimes succeed in getting things done they are not influencing for successful, long term outcomes. When you force, push, bludgeon, bully or harangue people against their will to do what you want, you have not created winning support. You have only created an atmosphere of mistrust around you and this will have a negative impact on your ability to influence. If you coerce someone, without taking their views or feelings into consideration, you will eventually fail as an influencer.

Others are far more willing to meet you halfway, or even completely, if they consider that you have understood, appreciated and acknowledged them. They may even end up agreeing to changes or actions that they wouldn't previously have contemplated, just because you have allowed them to feel good about making those choices.

What influences us?

Everything has the ability to influence us. The secret is to acknowledge that you can control the effect of its impact and the duration of the influence. Many allow themselves to be influenced without

147

bothering to consciously get involved and that is why such vast sums are spent on those twin powers of persuasion; advertising and marketing. They work!

List all the things that have influenced you over the last 24 hours, making sure that you have considered all the different forms of media, people, sounds, objects, sights and conversations.

The list will give you some insight about what you allow to influence you at a subconscious level, which is where you need to have more control. Notice how the message was presented to you as this will also give you greater understanding of the power of influencing.

SELF DIAGNOSTIC BOX
What has influenced me today?

Power, money, sex, religion, height, appearance, speech, status, intelligence, credibility, expertise, reputations and physique are all powerful influencers and you need to know which holds the most power over you to govern your choices.

To help you to find the things which might influence you fill in the table below which suggests some common influencing factors. The blank rows are for you to add in any others which have power over you. Spend time considering each one, honestly marking it out of 10. Use 10 for very powerful influencers all the way down to 0 if you are not influenced by it at all. An easy way to complete this task with the necessary degree of honesty is to identify some key influencers in your life, both positive and negative, and to think of them whilst working through the list. For example, when you attend a meeting, do you behave differently when the managing director is present? If you change the way you behave when the managing director is present, ask yourself, how much does my behaviour change on a scale of 0 to 10? Put the number in the right-hand column.

What is it about another person that influences the way I behave or respond to them?	0 to 10
Am I influenced or impressed by a person's **Power** (prime minister, managing director, manager, councillor etc.)?	
Am I influenced or impressed by a person's **Money** (lots of money—very rich)?	
Am I influenced or affected by a person's lack of **Money**?	
Am I influenced or impressed by **Males**?	
Am I influenced or impressed by **Females**?	
Am I influenced or affected by a person's **Religion**?	
Am I influenced or impressed by a person's **Height** (tall)?	
Am I influenced or impressed by a person's **Height** (short)?	
Am I influenced or impressed by a person's **Appearance** (clothes, hair, nails, shoes etc.)—appealing?	
Am I influenced or affected by a person's **Appearance** (clothes, hair, nails, shoes etc.)—not appealing, scruffy, dirty or old?	
Am I influenced or affected by someone who is **Ugly**?	
Am I influenced or impressed by someone who is **Good Looking**?	
Am I influenced or affected by someone who **Speaks** with appealing dialect, tonality, accent and speech patterns?	
Am I influenced or affected by someone who **Speaks** with a poor dialect, coarse or vulgar accents, bad grammar and/or speech impediments—not appealing?	
Am I influenced or impressed by someone's **Status**?	

What is it about another person that influences the way I behave or respond to them?	0 to 10
Am I influenced or impressed by someone's **Intelligence**?	
Am I influenced or affected by someone's **Lack of Intelligence**?	
Am I influenced or impressed by someone being labelled as an **Expert** in their field?	
Am I influenced or affected by someone who is **Fat**?	
Am I influenced or affected by someone who is **Thin**?	
Am I influenced or affected by someone who has a bad **Reputation**?	
Am I influenced or affected by someone who has a good **Reputation**?	
Am I influenced or affected by someone who has **Celebrity** status?	

If you have two or three factors with top scores, simply ask yourself which one really would have the most influence over you. Think of any acquaintances with that particular influencing factor as this will help you make the distinction. Now that you know what influences you and the level of power that these factors have over you, you can decide right now to control the influence or to allow yourself to be influenced. The important distinction is that you get to consciously choose and this will give you more flexibility during your negotiations.

Bridge building

There will be situations where influence is being applied and you become aware of the need to change what is happening, to effect a change to the scene for one that you are more comfortable with.

Rapport is the bridge over which all good communicating and influencing takes place. You can build rapport with mirroring and matching, simple questioning and good active listening. Appropriate focused responding will also help to build the bridge of rapport over which you can achieve powerful outcomes. There are more ways to build rapport in Chapter Ten, Neuro-Linguistic Programming Success.

Influencing and communication dynamics

When you influence others, whether this is face-to-face, over the phone or within a group at a summit conference, meeting, training, seminar or other gathering, it will be your ability to 'work the dynamics' that will affect the outcome. You will be using all the nuances of verbal and non-verbal communication at your disposal to create the impact you want instead of just letting things happen. You will be aware of the influence that others are having on the group dynamic and this will give you the clues to alter your approach should you need to

The view from the other side

Everyone see things differently and they also think their view is the right one. This means that they cannot understand why someone does or thinks of things differently from them—why would anyone want to do that?

The influencing skill is being able to look at a problem from another's

SELF DIAGNOSTIC BOX

What do I know about the person I want to influence?

151

vantage point and to make decisions on the way forward from that place. This will give you a great deal of information which you can use to influence them effectively. This is a much quicker and more effective method than trying to convince others that you are right and they are wrong.

Influence by status

You need the ability to deliberately raise and lower your status to stay in charge of, or to influence, a situation. The formal term for this is 'situational status profiling' and it is different from a standard hierarchical status because it incorporates more than just one person's position.

In other words, it is like the meeting where the person with the highest position within the company is not the person with the most influence on the attendees. Here is how you can become the influencer: you create a stakeholder map and use lobbying.

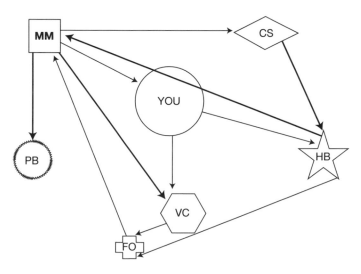

Your stakeholder map

Stakeholder mapping

Before you begin this procedure you need a well-formed idea of the outcome that you desire, as without this directional signpost you can neither map effectively nor influence to the best advantage. To create your stakeholder map you need to identify the key people that you need to influence and then decide how to influence them and the other strong influencers with accurate targeting. Your map will also tell you 'who influences whom' within the group and you can then draw up a strategy to ensure you have lobbied to the best of your abilities prior to any decisions being made.

To create your map:

1. Decide on your shape and put yourself in the middle of the map as above.

2. Decide on the type of shape you want for each influencer. Use different shapes for each person and put their initials into the shape. If you need absolute confidentiality, use a numbering system.

3. Now put the main influencers around you and use arrows to show the connections between all of you. The person the arrow is pointing at is the one who is influenced by the shape (person) from whence the arrow originated.

4. Show any secondary influencers' links to the relevant main influencer and, where necessary, label them so you keep track of who is influencing whom, i.e. FO influences MM the main influencer in the example above, even though FO is a subordinate to VC who does not influence MM. How could this happen? Well perhaps FO is a family member, friend or even an elicit lover of MM.

5. If one of your main influencers can be influenced by a secondary influencer from any of the lines of influence, use the codes to remind yourself that there may be some leverage you could use here and consider building a relationship with the secondary influencer for lobbying purposes.

Lobbying dovetail outcomes

This is a method to ensure that an outcome results in all parties believing they have achieved a win–win rather than win–lose or lose–win outcome.

Lobbying is an essential part of influencing and we do it all the time. You might not recognise it as this because the word is so strongly linked with politics. Here is a simple example of everyday lobbying.

A teenager wants to go to a burger joint and knows that his father is not keen on the family eating there. So he goes to his brother and gets him on board, then both of them go to the mother and suggest that instead of her cooking after a hard day at work, they could all go to the local burger joint. The mother realises she is being coerced into agreeing but still allows herself to go along with them. Now, when the teenager talks to his father he has enlisted all of the rest of the family. In other words, he has influenced the other main players against his main challenger to get the outcome he wants.

Within the meeting situation you can use a similar strategy. Enlist the other players on an individual basis prior to the meeting and then, during the meeting, propose a vote. Another way is to assertively ask the strongest influencer of your enlisted team to give their views on the subject during the meeting and then to support the view (your view) that they propose!

So few managers understand lobbying that using these techniques before most meetings will result in you building a reputation as a powerful influencer. You must take the time to have those pre-meeting satellite discussions with the other influencers to really impact on the outcomes.

At the beginning of this section the first sentence has a very important word which I would like you to identify now: 'This is a method to ensure that an outcome results in all parties believing they have achieved a win–win rather than win–lose, or lose–win outcome.'

The important word is 'believing' and I am sure you spotted it. Believing can be different from the reality and this is where influencing uses the element of perception changing. Once some-one believes something they will use commitment and consistency to confirm and support their belief.

Nine tools of influence

Below are nine different approaches to influencing, which will give you an influencing toolbox enabling you to select the best tool for the job.

1. **Influencing with 'because'.** When you understand the power of the word 'because' you will be amazed at how you can use it when influencing an outcome. In a 1978 research document by Langer, Blank and Chanowitz, an experimental study is reported where they observed how often library patrons would comply with a request: 'Excuse me, I have five pages. May I use the copy machine *because* I have to make copies?' as well as several variants of the same request. The researchers found that the redundant request ('I have to make copies') resulted in 93 per cent of people queuing to use the photocopier allow-ing the requester to use the copy machine first! When you use 'because' you will hugely increase your chances of a successful outcome. It is believed that the use of 'because' gives a reason and even if, as in the example, the reason is obvious and therefore redundant, peo-ple still want to comply.

    SELF DIAGNOSTIC BOX

    How can I use 'because' when influencing?

    In every form of communication where you require someone to do something, follow your request with a 'because' and you will dramatically increase your influence and effectiveness.

2. **Influencing with contrast.** Using contrast to influence means proposing something outrageous and then after the arguments have settled down, proposing something much more acceptable. The people you are influencing will be so grateful that you are not pushing for the original outrageous option that they will settle for, and support, your secondary option—which of course was your preferred outcome all the time. Some sales assistants in department stores use this technique to increase their sales. They spot a customer looking at jumpers in the low price range and start a conversation about cashmere and silk mixes being the 'all the rage these days'. Then they ask the customer if they have seen the new jumpers which are almost identical to the cashmeres but are less expensive. Before the customer knows it they are buying a medium priced jumper instead of the cheaper version which they had intended to buy. This works because (see above for how I am influencing you) the customer can stretch to the medium priced jumper but not the cashmere, and he or she goes away confused but happy.

    > **SELF DIAGNOSTIC BOX**
    >
    > What is the most outrageous proposal I can think of?

3. **Influencing with reciprocity.** This influencing technique uses emotional debt as the compelling reason for allowing oneself to be influenced. Reciprocity is the law of giving. When someone offers you a gift, you feel obliged to give them something in return. The key is to realise that the gift need not be tangible (although tangible is really powerful). For example, you may have an employee who is not working to maximum capacity and you know that, if you were to loan this person to another department, it could result in many favourable outcomes for you. You also need that department to use a different process to reduce the work of your own team by a third, but up until now the manager has been resistant to the change. You also know that this department is understaffed. To use this situation

to your advantage you press the pain button by mentioning the heavy workload that this department is straining under and then, in front of other managers, you offer your employee on loan to help them out. It does not matter if the gift is accepted or not, as once you bring up the new process you will be in a much stronger position to get the outcome you are looking for. I would also have lobbied the other main influencers before the meeting to increase my chances of success. Nevertheless, the law of reciprocity is so strong that in most cases it will work.

> **SELF DIAGNOSTIC BOX**
>
> What can I use that has little cost to me and great value to others?

4. **Influencing with social proof.** Large corporations use this all the time with celebrity endorsements of their products. If the celebrity is using the product then so will some members of society. Lobbying relies on this influencing technique. If you have lobbied the support of 75 per cent of the meeting attendees or 50 per cent of the strongest influencers and you call on them to vocalise their support or visually indicate it by show of hands, you are eliciting social proof which they are happy to demonstrate.

> **SELF DIAGNOSTIC BOX**
>
> Who do I know who is willing to give me a testimonial?

Testimonials are a great way of using social proof to influence as they imply word-of-mouth recommendation. I use testimonials in my own business and have many on my website. I send out a testimonial document with my information packs and I arrange for prospective customers to call the coaches that I have trained to 'see what they thought of the opportunity'. Of course, they receive an independent verbal testimonial.

If you are employed you can ask for testimonials from directors or senior functional managers. In the meeting in which you want to have influence, you 'name drop' the testimonial by saying: 'Sam Bloggs is fully behind this project and was only today extolling its virtue.' If you can get Sam Bloggs to email you with the testimonial, you can print off copies for the attendees. This adds strength to your proposal because the written word has more power to influence than the spoken word.

5. **Influencing with double binds.** The double bind influencing technique uses the simple word 'or' to affect the outcome. You need to be offering the other person the same thing with an 'or' in the middle of the two similar options—hence the term double bind. An example: you seek an appointment with someone who has yet to agree a date. You know that until you have secured the date the meeting will never take place. So you can say: 'Shall we settle on an appointment date now *or* jot down the time to get together.' This is strengthened

> **SELF DIAGNOSTIC BOX**
> How could I use the double bind to secure my outcome?

if you keep on talking, so the double bind is less obvious. A similar technique is used in the selling process and is known as an alternative close. You offer the customer delivery today *or* Thursday; the differentiation being that a double bind uses the same thing but the alternative close offers two different things. Both understand the power of the little word 'or'. Yet another use of 'or' is shown in the presumptive question; you presume that a customer is going to buy from you by asking, 'Would you prefer to pay by cheque *or* by credit card?'

6. **Influencing with commitment and consistency**. This influencing relies on the human need to feel internally consistent, even if, on the surface of things, it is against their own self-interest. Here is a simple example which you can test for yourself.

Go to a race track (any track) and do a random test of the attendees. Simply identify 10 people and ask them these questions:

a) Have you placed a bet on the 3.30 race (a race that has not taken place yet)? You are looking for 10 people who have not.

b) Ask all 10, if they placed a bet on the 3.30 race, do they believe their choice of horse/dog will win. Keep records of 'yes' and 'no' answers.

c) Wait until they have placed bets on the 3.30 and ask them the same question, 'Do you think you will win?'

You should notice that prior to placing any bets on the 3.30 race, your results will show that most of the punters say that they will not win. Yet, the same punters asked the same question after placing the bet will now say 'Yes', probably giving you 85 per cent or more saying 'Yes'.

Why the change? Well they have now made a commitment supported and strengthened by money. If they now say 'No' to the question, 'Do you think your choice will win?', they will appear stupid and inconsistent and so they will not go against their internal need for consistency.

SELF DIAGNOSTIC BOX

When have I done something just because I said I would, even when it was not in my interests?

When you want to influence always get the commitment first. The most effective way of doing this is to get agreement to small insignificant things along the way so that, when you need them to agree, a pattern or habit of agreement has already been set, making one more agreement a natural progression for them.

7. **Influencing with scarcity.** This powerful method of influencing relies on human psychology. The less there is of something the more desirable it becomes. So all you have to do is make what you are offering a rarity. When I go along to do a keynote speech I only take a few of my books with me (but I always have plenty of order forms) and, nearing the end of the talk, I will mention, or get the host (even more powerful—social proof) to mention, that I have a limited number of books with me and that those interested can buy them in the foyer at the end. I always receive orders for far more books than I can carry with me.

SELF DIAGNOSTIC BOX
How can I make scarcity work for me?

8. **Influencing with authority.** This is self-explanatory. If you have the authority you will be given the power to influence because of your position. Note that this may not be based on your expertise or competence but simply on your pecking order in the workplace.

9. **Influencing with credibility.** This means that if you can prove your credibility you will be given the power to influence naturally. How do you get

SELF DIAGNOSTIC BOX
How can I use authority or credibility to influence others?

credibility? Become an expert in a field, write a book, do talks, be consulted, go on radio or television as an expert. Once you are perceived to be the expert you will be given influence. You need to decide if this is worth the effort for the outcomes you desire.

The successful influencer uses all of the above ways of influencing and often employs several at the same time. You need to practise these skills until they become second nature. The easiest way to do this is to practise on family and friends without telling them what you are doing and before launching the techniques in an important meeting.

Easy influencing process

Taking charge of the influencing arena can be done by using a simple step-by-step process:

1. Create a shareholder map.
2. Decide on your lobbying strategy prior to event.
3. Establish instant rapport.
4. Ensure that the outcomes are set and aimed at win–win solutions.
5. Step into the shoes of the attendees in order to obtain their perspective.
6. Use perceptual models and flow charts to provide insights and options.
7. Ask effective focused questions to manage the interaction and establish real meaning.
8. Recognise and use the key elements of language (verbal and body) peculiar to each individual in order to motivate them towards your outcome.
9. Confirm outcome.

Dealing with contention

Sometimes during sensitive meetings you will encounter a controversial matter that causes friction and discord. It is impossible to get agreement to outcomes when discord is present so you must resolve this before moving to a conclusion. An effective approach when considering contentious issues is to look at them from three different perspectives to get multiple descriptions, and so to acquire more options in dealing with the situation and the people involved.

Contention resolution process

1. Identify all the areas about which you all disagree. I know this sound strange but often, once people start describing their disagreement, they can see the folly of it and change their minds in mid flow.
2. Ask each challenger to use one or two words as a title for their viewpoint.
3. Ask the attendees if they are committed to finding an agreed outcome.
4. If yes, draw three circles on the flip chart and label them with the titles (Stage 1).
5. Ask people to work in pairs to find the commonality between the three circles.
6. Join each circle with commonalities to the other circle. This should give you all ideas on ways forward (Stage 2).
7. Agree on the way forward.

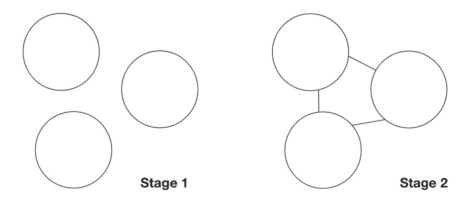

Stage 1   **Stage 2**

If at Stage 3, participants do not want to commit to finding an agreed outcome, dissolve the meeting and set a date for a further meeting. You now have a great opportunity to lobby and you know the position your opposition has on the matter. This puts you in a place of power. You need to design a lobby strategy and obtain social proof, preferably from an authority and credibility stance. You can also use some reciprocity when lobbying. When you resume the meeting, take with you a drawing of the three cir-

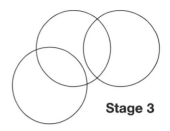

Stage 3

cles overlapping as in Stage 3 and offer your solution. Remember, after you have offered your solution, seek the opinions of the people who you know (because of your lobbing) will support you first. Ask all the supporters first, as this creates social proof, and then throw in your authority/credibility testimonial to add weight to the argument.

Tip

When dealing with difficult people, a phrase I often use is 'I noticed that …' and I describe the behaviour (not the character) in non-confrontational terms. For example, 'I noticed that you were uncomfortable with …' This is a simple model that is useful in trying to pre-empt difficulties or to bring a tricky situation to someone's attention in a neutral, non-judgemental way. Avoid the knee-jerk reaction that commonly arises by blame and concentrate on the effect that has (or hasn't) happened. This approach avoids blame and allows situations to move forward.

When going into an influencing event for the first time it is natural to feel a little apprehension. Remember, perception is reality, which makes perfect sense in the context of influencing. Therefore, it doesn't matter what is going on internally for you—if it isn't perceived by the other people, then it doesn't exist, other than in your mind.

An additional benefit of using your influencing skills well is that other people will enjoy being around you. You will create an exciting buzz or perception that good things happen when you are around. People will be attracted to you and this in turn will make your influencing easier.

Success Box

1. What influences you the most?

2. Complete your stakeholder map

3. Decide on an influencing strategy

4. Practise lobbying

5. Start using 'I noticed that ...'

Action I Will Take

Completed on:

/   /

Action I Will Take

Completed on:

/   /

Action I Will Take

Completed on:

/   /

Action I Will Take

Completed on:

/   /

Action I Will Take

Completed on:

/   /

Action I Will Take

Completed on:

/   /

Chapter Ten

Neuro-Linguistic Programming Success

Once you know how to use NLP tools and techniques you have some of the most powerful keys to success.

Synopsis

In this chapter, you will discover the reasons for using NLP to influence someone towards your outcomes. You will understand why you are successful sometimes and how to be more consistently successful.

It was a week before Annie Cheung's thirtieth birthday. It was also nine weeks since she had started looking for a job. She had deliberately stopped work following the birth of her daughter Amanda to be at home to look after her during the important early years. Now Amanda was eight and becoming more independent.

Annie's educational record was better than average and her CV was impressive because she had achieved rapid promotions at a relatively young age. These facts alone meant that she had been invited to several interviews. However, although she felt that she had performed well, none had resulted in a job offer.

It was also the end of a school term for Amanda and time for the annual parent and teachers' evening. She need not have worried for, like her mother, she was a bright student gifted with a sunny disposition.

Annie obediently did the rounds of the teachers who were seated around the edge of the school hall. She glanced up and read, 'Miss Brown – Drama'. After the usual favourable comments, Miss Brown said that there was something that Annie could do to help her daughter: 'We have all noticed that when Mandy is nervous, tense or angry, her voice takes on a stridency and high pitch that is most unattractive. That's why she is never given speaking parts in the school drama productions.'

Much later that night, relaxing in bed, Annie had a flashback to her own childhood in Hong Kong. Once again, she heard her own father telling her, and not for the first time, 'Annie, if you keep screeching like that you will have every cat in the island coming to investigate.' Could it be that people thought she still screeched, just like Amanda and those alley cats?

She got up and found her ancient cassette tape recorder and then amused herself for an hour or more, trying various readings and sounds and then playing them back. The next day she visited the library and carried home several books with chapters on voice training and breath control. She grinned to herself as she read how Britain's first female Prime Minister had been coached to modulate her voice from 'bitch pitch' to 'middle register' so that she could project an air of gravitas, strength and apparent wisdom.

Annie's best friend gave her a book as a birthday present. 'It is about something called NLP and it sure helped me in so many different ways,' she said. Annie read the book from cover to cover over the next couple of evenings and then again, more slowly, whilst making notes.

She had three interviews the following week. Just before each of them she smilingly visualised Miss Brown repeating her own father's words, she became conscious of her breathing rate and then, during the interviews, she gently applied the rapport building techniques that she had been reading about. She was offered all three jobs and wisely chose the one that was closest to home—it offered the highest salary too. Annie wrote in her diary: 'This cat stopped screeching and got the cream.'

Once you have the power to influence another person you have the key to success in achieving your outcomes. Neuro-Linguistic Programming (usually referred to as NLP) has been defined as 'the art and science of personal excellence'. At its simplest level, NLP is a series of techniques and procedures for coding human behaviour. It suggests how to use the information gathered in aiding the understanding of what people do and how they perform with excellence.

NLP is both an art and a science. The art component is how we make NLP personal to us when we practise it. The science component is based on detailed research of the methods and processes used by outstanding individuals in many fields to deliver outstanding results. I have already explained that, to be successful, you need to define what success means to you. NLP is an accelerated pathway to formulating your definition.

Background

NLP was identified and developed in the early 1970s, in the US, by John Grinder and Richard Bandler. Richard Bandler was a psychology student working with John Grinder, an assistant professor of linguistics at the same university. They studied and analysed the astounding results being obtained by top people in various therapy practices.

They hypothesised and then proved that any given procedure or conduct can be replicated and modelled. This led to the breakthrough reasoning that we can even control our automatic programmed responses to given situations and deliver predictable outcomes or results.

In practical terms and plain language, Bandler and Grinder showed that anyone can use straightforward NLP processes and use them to achieve excellent results in all their communications and personal development progress—including the achievement of success.

To give you a taste of NLP and to hopefully stimulate your own interest in further reading on the topic, I have selected just a few of the basic techniques here. Others are touched on in the individual chapters, where their use is more relevant. Do not be put off by the jargon because NLP really is rational, simple, proven, powerful and easy to use.

Rapport

In the first book of this series, *The Life Coaching Handbook*, I described rapport as: 'the bridge that we build between our clients and ourselves and over which all communication must pass'.

Rapport occurs naturally when we are striving to build a relationship and you not only need to be naturally good at building rapport but you want to excel in this skill if you seek true success in all areas of your life.

SELF DIAGNOSTIC BOX

How good am I at building rapport?

Great rapport is established in two main ways: with body language or with verbal language. In both instances you will be perceived by the other person as 'just like me'. This of course, can be read two ways. That person could be pleading for you to 'just like me' but, more likely, they are thinking that you are very similar to them. We all feel more comfortable with people who we believe are like us and NLP helps to create this mindset in the other person.

Body language

A quick way to build rapport is through body language. Rapport is a dance of synchronicity, of matched or mirrored movements and, when there is no rapport, there is no dance. Join the other person in their own dance if face to face or by matching their tone, pace and pitch when speaking over the phone. Care needs to be taken so that the procedure is invisible because there is a fine line between matching and mirroring and mimicking. The first two are acceptable and essential to building rapport. Mimicking, on the other hand, is disastrous and should be avoided at all costs.

As you might have guessed, mirroring is copying the other person as if you were looking into a mirror—they lift their right arm and you lift your left arm. Matching is doing the same thing—they lift their right arm and you do the same. Remember the dance analogy; it is smooth, natural and synergistic. You already do it naturally when you are with your friends and this is just an extension of that. Observe others who appear to be in a trusted, familiar or intimate relationship and note how they automatically match and mirror the movements of their partner. They sit in similar postures, they walk in step and they may even share facial expressions. A tip is to think of people as your friends as this will make the process seamless.

Matching breathing rate is the foundation for matching pace of speech. You cannot breathe slowly and speak quickly. We all blink our eyes at different rates and, sometimes, the more subtle approach of matching your client's blink rate is easier than changing your body position or matching their breathing. Facial expressions offer further opportunities to build rapport by mirroring. As you practise, start with a smile which is the best way to establish rapport.

The success factor here is apparent as soon as you become aware you are having communication difficulties with someone. Pay conscious attention to your body language and theirs. Adjust yourself by mirroring or matching the other person and you will quickly establish and sustain body language rapport.

Verbal language

The fastest way to build rapport with language is to use the same words as the other person. This sounds simple and it is. Care is needed because you only need to change one word to change the whole meaning for the other person.

John Grinder and Richard Bandler developed the theory that professionals in almost any field could increase the trust and rapport with

SELF DIAGNOSTIC BOX

Do I include the words I hear into my language patterns?

their client or trainee by using the individual's primary language system. They concluded this by listening to the words that the trainee used, along with their preferred speech patterns, and then they used exactly the same words and constructions in their own sentences, with phenomenal results.

Representational systems

Representational systems are simply the ways that all humans make sense of the world around them. It can be used to great effect in building rapport.

We all process information through our five senses and we store and retrieve information by using the same senses. Although we use all our senses, there are three commonly defined preferences or representational systems: visual, auditory and kinaesthetic. Most people tend to favour one of these.

The table opposite is intended to be used as a beginner's guide on each of the three main representational systems and can act as your starting point of recognition. There will be exceptions to the list of representational system identifiers below and you need to use your powers of observation, as well as listening and questioning, to assist you.

The key to building successful rapport is to identify the other person's preferred representational system and then to join them in it. Remember that 'people like people like themselves'. Have fun with this because you learn to adapt more quickly when you have fun learning the styles. The jump from visual to kinaesthetic is greater than from visual to auditory, and you will need to practise speeding up or slowing down so that when you change to another representational system, the changeover will be seamless, subtle and instantaneous.

Type of rep system	Some language identifiers	What to adapt to build rapport
Auditory	That *sounds* good I would like to *listen* *Tuned* in Manner of *speaking* *Word* for *word* *Rings* a bell	Let's *talk* to her Did you *hear* that? *Loud* and *clear* Within *hearing* Hidden *message*	Match tone, pitch and pace Use melodic rhythms and tilt your head occasionally Get into a relaxed mindset Breathe at medium pace from middle of body
Kinaesthetic	I can't get a *handle* on that We'd better get in *touch* *Hold* on to that idea Let me *walk* you through that idea *Cool, calm* and *collected* *Slipped* through my hand All *washed* up *Hand* in *hand* *Hot*-headed *Pull* some strings	Come to *grips* with *Hold* it! *Sharp* as a razor Start from *scratch*	Speak in a slow measured manner Breathe slowly from the bottom of your stomach
Visual	*See* you later I want to *look* at it *Picture* this It *appears* to me A *vision* in pink! *Photographic* memory	Let's *focus* on this It's a bit *hazy* *Watch* out! Did you *notice* that *Showing* off Pretty as a *picture*	Speak quickly Breathe quickly from the top of your chest Be sharp and energised/passionate

Reframes

Just as pictures on your wall are contained in a frame, we each frame our vision of the world; so in NLP parlance, a frame is 'the setting of the scene'. A reframe is simply 'changing the scene' by offering an alternative presentation. Reframing is a brilliant tool for escaping from being stuck in a rut of thinking.

You may be familiar with the well-used saying, 'Is the cup half empty or half full?' Ask yourself: 'How do I see the cup?' If you always look on the bright side of life you will be able

SELF DIAGNOSTIC BOX

Is my cup half empty or half full?

to spot the advantages and upsides in any situation. Conversely, if you always see the dangers, downsides or the negatives of an event, your reframing skills will help you transform your inner voice from negative to positive. A positive outlook is an essential component for success.

Notice what you say to yourself during the day. Try this example of a negative frame: your boss comes in and tells you to do something; what do you say to yourself?

a) She is picking on me because she does not like me
b) She is being lazy and is dumping on me again
c) She thinks I cannot do it and wants to show me up

If you think negatively during the day, work at reframing your inner voice. Instead of the examples above, you could say to yourself:

a) Great, she has chosen me as I am the best person for the job
b) Great, she is delegating to me so that I can learn
c) Great, she knows I can do the job

Here is an important point to remember. What is going on in your head only affects you; it does not affect the other person or the situation. In the above examples, you only changed your thinking and attitude and this will have made you more resourceful, less resentful, happier and more energetic. That is a pretty good pay off! It is easier to change your thinking than to change your boss and, anyway, whose day are you responsible for? It is your day, not hers!

You get to choose whether to make every day a success or a miserable failure. Chose to reframe—find the good, the positives, the upsides and the lessons to be learned from all difficult events. Soon you will find that even the bad times can be good. It is all in the reframe.

Metaprograms

I apologise for the jargon, but NLP has a unique language. Metaprograms are 'contextual specific filters' that we all use. Contextual means that they are neither definitive nor static. They change with the context or situation in which we find ourselves. In plain English, they are the ways that we see and interpret what goes on around us, and we do not use the same ones all of the time.

When you can identify a person's metaprogram in a given circumstance, you can influence that person. That is a pretty powerful statement of a pretty powerful ability so you really should not allow the language to put you off learning this bit.

I have only selected three easily observed metaprograms for this chapter, just to get you enthused and started on the journey. They are 'same/different', 'towards/away' and 'global/specific'. I recommend RAWPOWER research to take you to the next level.

Sameness or difference filters

Sameness filterers like the world to remain the same; difference filterers want the world to constantly change and be different. At the beginning of a conversation make sure you have both categories in your own language or ask questions planned to determine the other person's filters.

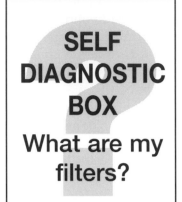

For example, with a new employee you could start with, 'Some of your goals will be the same as those which you have worked on before. We will also be looking at different ways to achieve them.' When you include both words in your opening sentences, you will be assured of arousing their interest, regardless of their preferred filter.

A quick way to recognise sameness or difference is by asking about the comparisons between their holidays of this year and last year. Sameness filterers will be inclined to say that it was the same place or same country and maybe even the same airline. Differencers would say it was different in all respects; destination, friends and time of the year.

You can change the word 'holiday' for a more appropriate or relevant topic. For instance, considering their job, home or car will give you the information that you require to find the distinction. When dealing with sameness filterers, fill your language, emails and reports with things that are the same or similar to those that they already understand.

When dealing with difference filterers, use things that are different from their previous experience. Always look for events or things that have variety and point out how each event and outcome will differ from those previously encountered.

Towards and away filters

Towards filterers are goal motivated; they like to achieve, attain and prioritise. Away from filterers recognise all too well what should be avoided and they are motivated to move away from problematic situations. To identify whether a person filters towards or away in a particular context, ask, 'What do you want from this meeting?'

Towards filterers will talk about wanting to gain things or to achieve and move forward. They will have a list of things to do and are animated and excited about the prospect of a new challenge. Encourage the enthusiasm and talk about new directions.

Away from filterers want to move away from their current job, partner, life and problems. They will not be inspired or motivated by thoughts of change. Show how they can easily get away from their painful situation. Support them by continuously reinforcing the benefits of leaving behind their troubles and how you can help.

Global and specific filters

The easiest way to understand this metaprogram is to think of the forest and the trees. Does the person like the global big picture (the forest) or specific details (the trees)? Global filterers want overviews, concepts and abstracts, whilst specific filterers like to deal with sequences in a step-by-step format and they need to know every small detail.

To recognise the difference between global and specific, simply ask any open question and listen for the reply. Your specific filterers will respond by giving you lots of details, your global filterers will respond with a very short focused answer. The power for your communication is to identify the filter and match the response. Give a lot of information to the specific filterers and a brief overview to the global filterers and you will be building bridges of rapport.

Just remember that people filter information differently and this will change according to the context. You need to listen and identify which filters they are using and then use the same filters to connect with them.

Metaphors

Metaphors are stories and sayings with symbolic significance and in this context I am discussing the metaphors that we tell ourselves. These metaphors can offer us good or bad choices and they can open up different ways of approaching problems, leading to new resources for resolving them. Metaphor telling has been the preferred method of imparting information for generations. Stories told of heroes and villains, good and bad and right and wrong. The great religious books of all faiths are metaphors giving guidance on how the followers should live their lives, what beliefs and values they should hold dear.

Metaphors can be extremely powerful and it is easy to construct one. Your imagination and creativity are the only limits to your metaphor skill. Once you become aware of them, you will realise that you frequently use metaphors to paint a graphic picture that is certainly not literal. For example, you have probably heard someone or yourself say, 'Life is an uphill struggle' or 'Life is a wonderful journey'.

If you can relate too 'Life is an uphill struggle' and similar metaphors, you will tend to focus on problems. If you decide (and you can do so right now!) to switch to positive metaphors, you will change your focus and eventually your results.

A great way to gain inspiration, motivation and success through metaphors is to read, listen to or watch inspirational stories. These can be related to the areas of your life where you want to improve your successes or they can simply be inspirational. The key is to change your thought patterns to give yourself greater options and alternatives.

All the stories at the beginning of each chapter in this book and at the beginning of the chapters in *The Business Coaching Handbook* are metaphors. The metaphors were specifically constructed to give the reader insight into the topic. Some of the metaphors tell the story by using the main character to give everyday examples of how the techniques within the chapter can be used.

Modelling

Modelling is as old as the hills and we are all practised in the art. From the moment of your awareness in this world you started to model behaviours of the people around you. As a child you learned to talk, walk and eat cleanly by being a mimic and modelling your parents.

Mimicking is straight copying; modelling is more than this. You need to select the skill you wish to acquire, find an appropriate role model and then you can either achieve the skill by doing the same thing in the same way or a more powerful modelling process is researching their motivations and development of that skill. To become a comedian, for example, you would find the best and most respected comedian to study. You cannot simply copy his material and performances as this would be unethical.

You can read, watch and listen to all the output that he/she has produced. Listen to interviews, visit websites, watch the biography channel, read autobiographies and biographies and join any fan groups or supporters' newsletters. Find out what is important to your model. What does your model believe about themselves and their performance? What values does your model have, what is most important to the model and what rules (rule book) control the way they think and behave? If you obtain all this information you will have a blueprint for that skill. All you need to do is to adopt the values, beliefs, behaviours and rules governing the model's skill and you should be able to replicate the success. You will need to practise, evaluate and adjust until you have mastered the skill to the level of your model.

> **SELF DIAGNOSTIC BOX**
>
> Who would be a good role model for my next skill?

You may want to contact your model and see if he/she is prepared to let you shadow him/her—this is more acceptable within the corporate or business world. The shadow process is often used by mentors to shortcut the learning of a particular way of behaving or a specific skill set. Shadowing is where you act like a shadow and go everywhere your model goes for a day, week or agreed timeframe. The key is that a shadow only speaks if spoken to, does not intrude and simply observes. Before you approach a prospective model, consider what you could offer as an inducement (service, product or gift). Answer their doubts with absolutely honesty and explain your motives for wanting the skill.

Modelling is a powerful way to quickly increase your skill set. Your model will have already made the mistakes so that you don't have to. You really can shortcut your route to success by standing on the shoulders of such giants. (Did you notice the metaphor?)

Neuro-Linguistic Programming is a powerful set of tools and techniques to increase your chances of success and here I have only covered a few of them. Again I recommend RAWPOWER to expand your skills and expertise in this fascinating topic. Once you have the power to influence another person you have one of the keys to success in achieving your outcomes. NLP will give you tools to influence with elegance.

Success Box

1. Practise building rapport

2. Discover your preferred representational system by reading a book on NLP

3. Practise reframing on family and friends

4. Spot the metaprograms during the next meeting that you attend

5. Listen to your metaphors

Action I Will Take

Completed on:

/   /

Action I Will Take

Completed on:

/   /

Action I Will Take

Completed on:

/   /

Action I Will Take

Completed on:

/   /

Action I Will Take

Completed on:

/   /

Action I Will Take

Completed on:

/   /

Chapter Eleven

Interview Success

Know specifically what prospective employers are looking for in a candidate and you will make it difficult for them to choose anyone else.

Synopsis

This chapter covers an effective method to increase your chances of success getting a job interview and securing the job. The techniques can also be used in any other interview situation.

Roger Kenwood found himself in a strange position. As a professional troubleshooter he would occasionally assume a temporary, or interim, management role. This time around it had been agreed that his managerial duties should become a permanent post and it fell to Roger to interview his own successor before moving on to new challenges and assignments.

He shortlisted four possible candidates from the stack of applications that landed on his desk before the advertised closing date. Any that arrived after the deadline were simply not considered. He had been appalled to receive one that was badly handwritten on headed paper from the individual's current employer and that arrived in a franked company envelope. So much for the 'honesty and attention to detail' that this person had listed under their personal attributes!

Two of Roger's chosen applicants then contacted him to say that they had already found alternative employment so he was left with two and, to avoid any possible embarrassment, he set their interviews for different days.

Joe Baker arrived sweating, carrying a plastic supermarket bag of papers, and was ten minutes late. Roger immediately noticed that Joe's shoes hadn't been polished for several weeks, that his shirt collar was grubby and that his badly knotted tie had a few stains of indeterminate origin. As Joe took a seat, Roger glanced over the CV to refresh his memory.

As he did this, Joe immediately went into talk mode where he blamed anyone but himself for his lateness, his previous employers for not recognising his good qualities and the world economy for the fact that he had been out of work for three months. This was before Roger had even asked a single question and, as he waited for a pause in the stream of nervous chatter, he noticed that Joe's entire body language had a hangdog look of failure. Out of respect, he went through a few prepared questions anyway. He had set aside one hour for the interview but brought it to a premature close after just 25 minutes.

Mark Good was the other candidate. He had arrived at the offices ten minutes ahead of time and was chatting cheerfully with the receptionist. When Roger greeted him he received a firm hand-shake, great eye contact and a friendly smile. Mark was smartly dressed without being dapper and Roger noted that his hair had that look that only good quality barbers can achieve. Roger later admitted that he was ready to offer the position within the first ten seconds.

Mark answered every question fully yet briefly and to the point; he asked a few very appropriate questions of his own and was able to amplify some points from his CV without hesitation. Roger was even surprised to hear himself agreeing to a salary which was at the higher end of the scale advertised and also to accommodating Mark's imminent holiday arrangements. After Mark had left, Roger allowed himself a satisfied smile. He had found a worthy successor and had extended his own assignment by a few weeks too, thanks to Mark's holiday plans. It had been a good and productive after-noon's work.

I have always been asked to attend interviews based on my cur-riculum vitae (CV) and, once I understood the secrets of the interviews, I was always offered the positions that I applied for. I believe this is all down to preparation and planning.

I was very fortunate that my first commercial position was as an executive recruitment officer in Britain's largest employment agency. This opportunity gave me valuable insights into the secrets of getting the job you want. I am going to share some of that knowledge and experience with you so that you can improve your own interview techniques and increase your percentage of job offers.

Normally, to be invited for an interview, you will have sent your details in one format or another and these details will have been appraised. In most cases a CV is your first contact with the company or employer.

What is a curriculum vitae?

Well, the words are Latin for 'life story', which, in the old days, would have been what it contained as back then people did not change jobs as frequently as they do today. These days it may be called a résumé, which is pronounced 'raysumay'.

What do you want to achieve with your CV?

The most important thing to understand about the CV is that it is your marketing brochure or sales document and it should promote your qualifications, skills and experience. Many job seekers create one CV and use it for all the jobs they apply for, and therefore completely miss its objective. You must see each version of your CV as a completely unique document which highlights your qualifications, skills and experiences *in the context of the vacancy that you are applying for*. Although the 'one size fits all' approach may sometimes land you an interview, keep track of the percentage of 'no thanks' responses to see the true results.

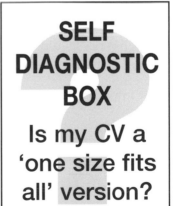

SELF DIAGNOSTIC BOX

Is my CV a 'one size fits all' version?

Look at it from the employer's point of view

Having been originally trained in the recruitment business, and over the years holding many senior executive positions, I have an astute insight as to what is required at an interview and throughout the recruitment process from interview to job offer.

Most managers or employers are very busy people and have to fit recruitment around a 'proper job'. This means that they will be time tight and ruthless with CVs and will select only those which match the job requirement. I would typically have between 50 and 100 CVs to read for one vacancy. I would always do a speed selection first, where I would glance at each one for presentation, layout and interest. If the CV did not grab my interest, stimulate further reading and have a clean, clear layout with easy to read font, it would be put on the scrap pile. It would take about 15 to 30 seconds to make this decision. Think about that for a moment—less than half a minute for your CV to work! This means that you need to make sure that yours includes *all* of the following.

1.   It should be typed in a clear font on good quality paper.
2.   It has to include emboldened headings, which could be underlined.
3.   It is succinct and only two A4 pages long.
4.   It lists an easily identifiable skills set on the first page.
5.   It has wide margins and a well spaced line layout.
6.   It has no spelling mistakes.

Remember, you only have a few seconds to make an impression. To do this you really do need to write a unique CV for every job you apply for and, if you cannot be bothered, someone else will and they will get the interview.

Research is the key

Make time to do your research as this will stand you in good stead for both your CV and for the interview. You need to have a copy of the job advertisement to hand and, if that does not give you enough information, call the company and ask for a copy of the job description and then, whilst you are on the phone, ask for a copy of their annual report. This is important because you will discover the names of managing directors/chief executive officers, their message to the sharehold- ers, the last year's profits and market share, the products, new products or projects, the vision and mission statements and lots of other important information to use at the interview.

Also, search the trade journals, business press, internet and all the company marketing materi- als. You will need to have an understanding of the company structure so that you know the progression routes and also the major successes of the company and milestones in its recent history.

> **SELF DIAGNOSTIC BOX**
> **What do I know about the companies I want to work for?**

Types of CV

There are two types of CV: the older sequential or chronological CV and the newer skills-based format, which is now preferred by most companies. The sequential or chronological version has, as the name suggests, a layout of everything in date order. As this can lack lustre and energy, I recommend the skills-based option, which I believe gives you a greater chance of success. The key to either is to keep it simple, containing only the important details that match the job description from the employer's point of view. Imagine you are the employer: it is your job—what would you be looking for? Remember that if you do not tell them what you can offer, they do not know it—you have to tell it because employers are not clairvoyants. There is no place for humility or modesty when compiling your CV.

Tips

1. Start with personal details, name, contact numbers and address etc. I do not recommend that you include your date of birth because, when I was interviewing, if there was no date of birth I would quickly look at the employment history. This means that your important skills will be looked at first and therefore give you a better chance of getting on the interview pile. You need to make the decision as to what personal details you want to include.

2. Include a 'statement of purpose' of what you stand for. Make this attention grabbing and stated in a couple of sentences. Match it to the vacancy.

3. Skills summary—amplify your skills which are appropriate to the job.

4. Brief work history—companies, jobs, dates, main achievements.

5. Summary of qualifications—brief and relevant.

6. Professional memberships, voluntary activities and hobbies. Again, select the most relevant. If you are applying for a sales position, your membership of networking groups, professional institutes and sports organisations will all convey the message that you have a network of contacts.

7. Remember, if you are not impressed by your achievements, why should the reader be?

Keep to two pages of A4. If you are applying for a highly skilled post you may want to attach a second more detailed CV (think of the exercise as if you were writing a business report where you have the executive summary followed by the supporting details).

If you have been published also attach the relevant copies, list speaking engagements, positive media exposure and any further supporting information. The key is to have the summary CV for the initial selection process and the more detailed sheets of sup-porting evidence which may be required for specialist expertise.

The key is clarity and matching—providing clear uncluttered information that matches the requirements of the job. That's it! Nothing more is necessary because if they want to know more, they will ask during the interview.

Application forms

Take your time and treat an application form with as much respect as a unique CV because it is just as important.

Tips

1. Photocopy the blank application form and fill the copy in first. This will concentrate your mind and if you make any mistakes it does not matter.

2. Once you have filled in the photocopy leave it overnight and reread the following day as you will always find something you forgot to add or missed from the job advertisement.

3. Make sure you match the job requirements as you fill in the form. Then check that you have put all your relevant skills, experience and qualifications somewhere on the form.

> **SELF DIAGNOSTIC BOX**
>
> **How much time do I spend filling in application forms?**

4. Never put 'see attached CV'. Always fill in their boxes and then attach your CV as an added extra should they have the time and inclination to read it (unless they specifically tell you not to).

5. Write in black ink in neat handwriting or better still type it or fill it in online. You need to have clear, neat and easy to read writing.

6. Take a final photocopy of the completed form so that you can recall what you said and take this with you to the interview.

Remember that the employer has many forms to read through so make sure your importantly matching skills are at the top of the relevant boxes.

Covering letter

It is essential to include a correctly laid out covering letter of one A4 page as it portrays a professional approach and gives you an added opportunity to sell and highlight your skills in relation to the job requirements.

Tips

1. Ensure you address the letter to the decision maker, taking care to spell their name correctly and therefore it will arrive on her/his desk.

2. State the job you are applying for at the top of the page.

3. Make it encouraging to the reader because it has relevance to the job.

4. If you send an exploratory letter and CV, make sure both are targeted. For example, 'The skills set I have would be well matched for your ... department because I have ... experience.'

5. State why you want to work for this particular employer.

6. Point to one or two key skills on your CV that the reader needs to be aware of, which happen to be the two major skills required to excel in the job.

7. Give indications of times you would be available for interviews.

8. Thank the reader for spending the time to read your letter and CV.

Make sure you keep a copy of all the documents that you send to each company along with all the research, any details of telephone conversations and the names of people you have spoken with.

The interview

The interview is about presenting the authentic you in the best possible light where the interview is enjoyable, interesting, stimulating and informative for you and the interviewer.

Before you attend

You need to prepare fully for interviews as they are the platform for your success.

SELF DIAGNOSTIC BOX

Did I really enjoy the last interview I attended?

It is useful to create an interview checklist that you can tick off on the day of the interview. As well as ensuring that you have everything in place, it gives you a boost of confidence that you are ready to go!

Research all the information that you have gathered about the company, select the most important and learn the facts. I always knew a potential employer's vision and mission statements, their last financial year's net profits and the targets for the current financial year. Also, some other facts such as the name of the CEO and MD, any parent or group companies, recent media exposure on the industry or profession in general, and any other interesting snippets of information. I would always find a way to skilfully and artfully introduce the information that I had researched to indicate that I was interested enough to do the research. Make sure you have a copy of the company annual report and take it with you to the interview.

Prepare your answers to the most common questions you expect to be asked and have specific examples with dates, facts and figures to support your answers. If you have many examples, you can prepare handouts which cover the details and be ready to explain one or two of the examples.

If you are required to do a presentation at the interview it is absolutely essential you rehearse out loud and practise until you can deliver it in your sleep. Remember, if they have asked for a 20-minute presentation, you must deliver a 20-minute presentation. Not a minute less or a minute more. Never overrun your time as you will be seriously penalised.

The only way to know how long your presentation lasts is to say it out loud and time it. Do this standing up in front of a mirror so you can check your overall look. If you are using presentation equipment make sure you know how it works and that you have supporting printed materials which you can leave with the interviewing panel and use if the equipment fails. Save these printed materials until the end of the presentation or interview. You want them to listen to you instead of reading whilst you are speaking. Make it exciting, passionate and interesting for your audience.

Set up a confidence anchor and any other positive emotional anchors you feel you might need to give you a boost on the day. Chapter Four, Emotional Success, has the steps for setting up a confidence anchor which you can adapt for any of the other emotional positive states you wish to recall during the interview. Remember to check that the anchor works for you before you leave for the interview.

Prepare the questions you would like to ask. On the first interview, avoid questions about salary increases, bonuses, packages and healthcare as these will be given to you or you can ask for them at a later stage.

Important last-minute preparations

Make sure you know and triple check the date, time and location of the interview. Always check again against your calendar or diary because it is easy to have convinced yourself it is on a certain date/time/location and find that you were mistaken. Check to avoid silly mistakes and call the company to verify your appointment on the day of the interview. Whilst checking your paperwork put aside any certificates that you were asked to take along to the interview.

SELF DIAGNOSTIC BOX

What is on my interview checklist?

Make sure you know how you are going to get to the location. Have some contingency plans and add an extra 20 to 30 minutes on to the normal travel time. It is better to be early than late. Carry a mobile phone just in case of enforced delays so you can alert the interviewer.

Your appearance must be appropriately smart, clean and well-groomed. Your hair needs to be clean, brushed and well cut. Your nails must be scrubbed and, if female, all nail polish should be chip free and the nails of an even length. Shoes should be clean and non-scuffed. Teeth need to be clean, food free and your breath should not smell.

On arrival ensure that the receptionist knows who you are and who you are going to see, and then visit the restroom to do a last minute check of your appearance. Then remind yourself that you have been called for an interview and therefore they must already see you in a positive light and set off your anchored positive emotional states. Smile and imagine that you are exactly what they are looking for and tell yourself you are ready to WOW them!

Remind yourself before the interview that there are no absolute right answers to questions you will be asked. It is also worth reminding yourself that the interviewer's objective is to fill the advertised post. In other words, they have as much interest in offering you the job as you have in wanting it!

Tricky questions you might be asked	Suggestions on how you could respond
What are the reasons for wanting to leave your current employment?	You need to be careful how you answer this question because criticising an employer is a flag to the interviewer. They will consider you as a potentially difficult employee regardless of the situation. You will not be able to justify criticism of your employer in a satisfactory manner no matter what you say. Change the negative to a positive statement; for example, 'I am looking for additional responsibility/new challenges/new opportunities that are limited where I am at present due to restrictions in (growth plans/promotional opportunities/size of company etc.).' Follow this with positive statements about the interviewing company where you believe they will be able to offer you the challenges you are looking for.
Why do you want to work for our company?	If you have done your research you will be able to easily answer this question. Things like: your progressive approach to XYZ, your leading edge technology, you are the market leaders and a company to aspire to work for, your creative innovative products.
Where do you see yourself in five or ten years' time?	A safe way to answer this is to keep your answer non-specific. Example: 'I would like to be regarded as an accomplished professional in my field of expertise.'
What style of management do you prefer or excel under?	You should already have an idea of the management style of this company from your research and it will give you indicators of your answer. If you are not sure here is another generic response example: 'I work well with guidance and a framework, where I am encouraged to contribute both supervised and autonomously to the success of the team.'

Tricky questions you might be asked	Suggestions on how you could respond
What are your greatest accomplishments?	Remember to select work-related examples that, wherever possible, are directly related to the type of things you would be doing in the new role. A great opener to this question is to start by saying, 'I feel my greatest accomplishments are yet to come,' smile and then continue with an example to demonstrate your skills in relation to the role.
What do you consider your most important strength?	Select a suitable characteristic relevant to the job role. If the job requires strong teamwork mention this and give an example. When answering this type of question always relate it to job requirements, give a brief example and deliver it with confidence and assertiveness. Be congruent with your answer.
What are your weaknesses?	You must prepare for this question beforehand and select something generic which will not impede your performance or contribution. For example, 'I tend to get absorbed in tasks, which means I sometimes leave work late' or 'Supporting team members in front of my own promotion'. You could use the desire for knowledge or other veiled strengths presented as weakness. They are not looking for a self-confessional only that you do not consider yourself beyond guidance. You may be asked for examples, so make sure they are also prepared.
How long would it take for you to make a contribution the company?	This is a question that needs a question: 'What project or area do you think needs a rapid contribution or that you want me to get involved in?' With this question, you have embedded the fact they want you to get involved. If this approach does not work simply follow up with the speed with which you made a contribution in your current company.

Tricky questions you might be asked	Suggestions on how you could respond
Why should we employ you?	Be confident as you answer this question because, if you are not confident, you cannot expect the interviewer to be confident in offering you the post. Identify two skills you have which match the requirements and explain how having these skills combined with enthusiasm and passion are the top reasons to employ you. I mentioned *top* because I anticipate they will ask you for the other reasons. This gives you a second opportunity to sell your other skills, attributes and characteristics.
How do you respond to pressure?	Avoid the temptation to simply say 'well'. See this as another selling opportunity. You could say that you find pressure stimulating and see it as an indicator that some extra planning and time management techniques may need to be applied to the situation.
What is your description of teamwork?	If you have read Meridith Belbin's books on teamwork you could mention his ideas and, this way, you would be considered as well-read and serious about work advancement. Remember, if the role requires that you work within a team the interviewer is looking for an answer which will add to the cohesion of the team and a contribution to the team which will enable them to reach their objectives.
What salary package are you looking for?	This is an awkward question if you have not prepared for it. Research the market rate for this type of job and then state that the average market rate is between X and Y and as you would be looking to make a rapid contribution and have # years' experience you would expect to get £# or even £# plus five per cent.

Tricky questions you might be asked	Suggestions on how you could respond
What is the most difficult problem you have had to deal with?	Understand that this question is looking to discover your analytical skills and your professional approach. If you already use a recognised methodology such as Edward de Bono's *The Six Thinking Hats* explain briefly how you used this approach on a specific problem. It is always more impressive if you can state the methodology you used plus a brief successful example.
What do you think your references would say about you?	This is show time! If they didn't hear it—you didn't say it, so make sure you know exactly what you are going say. Be succinct and focused and add some humour. Add any useful skills that have not been touched on during the interview. It is also a good time to announce the values you share with the company.
How do you spend your non-working time?	What you say must match your CV or the application form. There are two things to consider here. The first, you need to show contribution to society and also have a health regime. The second, if you have too many or are a little too enthusiastic about hobbies you may be considered as having a lack of commitment to work. Aim for a reasonable balance.

Questions you might ask

You will be asked if you have any questions and it is essential to have questions ready, because asking focused incisive questions conveys interest in the company and the position. Have a small list of questions and ensure that you do not ask any questions where the answer was already covered in the interview as this shows a lack of attention and poor listening skills.

Why has this position become vacant?	What training or induction programmes are available to new starters?
How many people are in the team?	What is the reporting structure?
What are the KPIs (key performance indicators) of the role?	What is the progression path and timeline?
What current competitive challenges does the company face?	What key challenges have the team surmounted in the last 12 months?
What are the current team targets and are you on track to meet them?	How has the interview gone?
What obstacles does the team encounter whilst working towards the targets?	What are the next steps? (You are looking for a decision date if possible.)

Things to consider

Enthusiasm is infectious and will show you at your best. Turn up the volume on the areas of your background which closely match the job and turn the volume down on the rest. If you are nervous you must still make eye contact and communicate clearly. This can be achieved by rehearsal prior to the interview on the answers that might come up and the ones you want to ask. Rehearsal is a critical success factor not only in job interviews but also for any other performances you have to make.

Another way of overcoming nerves is to consider it your personal responsibility to make the interviewer feel comfortable and to look after him/her. This allows you to considerately answer the questions and focus your attention externally instead of internally. It is always useful to have some anecdotes, past triumphs and humorous stories, all of which have a successful outcome, ready and rehearsed just in case you need them. If you are interested in the position tell the interviewer this at the end of the session prior to asking what happens next.

Things to avoid

Derogatory comments about competitors and current or previous employers are an absolute no-no! I cannot emphasise this strongly enough. No employer wants to offer a job to a moaning Minnie who could turn into a nightmare employee. They will not take the risk, so keep your comments or complaints about others to yourself at all times.

Avoid arrogance, which is also a turn off, and so are comments such as, 'It is written in the CV/application form.' The reason the interviewer is asking the question may be to see how you handle obvious questions and to demonstrate how you could interact within a team of mixed abilities.

Never lie during an interview although you can be judicious with the truth. However, if you are not asked you need not tell. If you are asked, and have disasters in your work history, it is good to acknowledge one and very *briefly* relate the details and what you have learned from the experience. It is always important to mention what you have learnt from mistakes as this shows humility and intelligence, which are great assets for new recruits.

Defensiveness will harm your chances of success. If you do not know the answer or do not have the appropriate skill, admit it and follow this with an example in the past where you overcame a skills need by attending training events or having coaching sessions.

After the interview

Analyse your performance immediately after you return and make notes on what you felt went well and what you could improve on in the future. If you have not been contacted after the selection deadline date, call the company and ask for the results. If you are not successful ask this question: 'Please tell me what one area I could improve in my interviewing technique?'

If you would like to work for the company, say this during the refusal telephone call and confirm by letter. Write a letter to the interviewer (copy to the Human Resources department) and thank him/her for taking the time to interview you and for providing a welcoming and relaxing environment. State that although you were unsuccessful for this position, as you mentioned in the interview, you really are very eager to become an employee and please could they advise you of any future vacancies your skill set could be appropriate for. Include a stamped addressed envelope to show that you mean what you say.

The panel interview

Panel interviews usually consist of two or more interviewers and they can all sit behind a long desk with your chair in the middle opposite. Mentally prepare for this scenario. It will not be as daunting if you have already visualised the process. Also, this type of interview uses different types of play off techniques—either the simple, with each interviewer taking turns asking you questions, or the good guy/bad guy where one asks pleasant easy to answer questions and another interviewer asks the tricky ones. A panel interview has been nicknamed a 'tag-team interview'. This type of interviewing technique is primarily used to determine how well you cope with stress and how you interact

SELF DIAGNOSTIC BOX

How do I prepare for a panel interview?

with different people, especially your manager, work colleagues, or both.

In your answers, include the person who sometimes sits silently in the corner or at the end of the table. They may just be taking notes but, equally, they may be the one who has the most input when the group discusses your performance.

Preparing for a panel interview is much the same as above and should include the following.

1. Research the company and the job description.
2. Memorise your CV/application form.
3. Rehearse talking about your experience, accomplishments and skills.
4. Prepare and rehearse meaningful questions to ask.
5. Be appropriately smart, clean and well-groomed.

Respond initially to the panel interviewer who asked the question and, as you continue to respond, acknowledge the others on the panel by making individual eye contact. Remember to address the whole panel because they will all be deciding on your suitability.

The group interview and group games

Group interviews usually mean you will be interviewed with other applicants at the same time. The simplest group interview can take the form of a company presentation followed by open discussions and question and answer sessions. This gives the interviewers a chance to initially screen candidates. They will be observing how you behave and if you stand out from the other candidates. Interviewers will also be taking note of the succinct and focused questions that you ask, which will show you have done your research and are serious about joining their company.

In some group interviews there may be activities that simulate a work environment by creating teams from the applicants and giving each group a work-related or hypothetical situation to resolve. Do not allow this team set-up to deflect you from remembering you are being individually scrutinised, listened to and that notes will be taken on your performance. What skills they are looking for will be determined by the positions available and usually include interpersonal, influencing, communication, leadership, teamwork, organisational, improvisational, feedback acceptance/approach, conflict resolution and stress control.

I would recommend that you aim to be among the leaders and take an active role rather than becoming an observer. Sometimes these scenarios have best possible solutions and it is easy to become involved in the context of solving the problem instead of remembering the importance of showing that you have the attributes required for the job you are applying for.

Take care with this type of interview and never lose sight of the skill set the job description requires. Adapt to show that your skills match what is required, regardless of the confusion that may ensue during the activity/game. At the end of the activity you may be asked to present with the rest of your team or on your own. Remember never to criticise other participants nor attribute blame; accept the outcome and make rational appraisal for improvements on a team level. The presentation is an opportunity to show your skills and a platform to sell yourself.

A tip for group interviews is to research the most popular team-leading games for businesses in order to familiarise yourself with the expected outcomes.

Badly organised panels

Sadly, you may be interviewed by a badly organised panel where you are pulled from pillar to post with non-sequential questioning and hostile attitudes. If you can find out from the Human Resources department the names and company positions of the people on the panel, and who will have the final decision, you will know who to pitch to. If this is not forthcoming you will just have to maintain your confidence and perform at your best.

A tip in handling this type of situation is to take longer than normal to answer the questions (pause a fraction longer than normal for you), lower your tone and slow down your pace. This has two effects; it sends a strong message to your subconscious that you are in control of reducing your nerves and it conveys to the panel that you consider their questions warrant serious consideration.

For those with little or no interview experience

If you have children or young adults with little or no interview experience, you can increase their chances of interview success enormously. You will need a friend that your 'candidate' has never met before and who has an office that can be used, perhaps after normal hours.

You will brief your friend beforehand with the points to be raised as he conducts a mock interview with your candidate who will attend at the appointed time, just as if this was for a real job. You will be there yourself, but not actually be in the interview room. As soon as the mock interview is over, ask your friend to give you and your candidate together, some honest feedback about his or her strengths and weaknesses during the interview along with practical suggestions for improvements.

Think of it as a rehearsal in a friendly but formal environment where there is no outcome other than adding experience and, probably, allaying nerves and fears.

For those who have a long work history

You may be justifiably proud of your long track record. However, remember that, from your interviewer's perspective, much of this will be ancient history. By all means answer any direct questions that you may be asked but otherwise avoid the past. Focus on recent achievements first. Be guided by the interviewer's body language and, as soon as you detect signs of boredom, stop talking.

You would be amazed how many job candidates (usually the more mature ones) get through almost to the point where a position is about to be offered and who then talk themselves right through it and out the other side with resultant disappointment.

In every situation

The important things to remember about being successful at interviews are: to do extensive research, to be fully prepared, to memorise your CV and application, to rehearse your answers, to rehearse your questions and to enjoy yourself.

Success Box

1. Write a unique CV for every new position you apply for

2. Keep a copy of all the paperwork

3. Have a checklist for the interview

4. Rehearse, rehearse, rehearse

5. Follow up all interviews

Action I Will Take

Completed on:

/   /

Action I Will Take

Completed on:

/   /

Action I Will Take

Completed on:

/   /

Action I Will Take

Completed on:

/   /

Action I Will Take

Completed on:

/   /

Action I Will Take

Completed on:

/   /

Chapter Twelve

Career Success

Success in your career needs to be planned and activated,
not left to chance.

Synopsis

In this chapter, you will discover ways to improve your success within your current career and will be given some ideas for looking at alternative careers.

Bill Fisher was experiencing a slow death by suffocation and frustration. When he joined this national organisation it seemed that there was ample room for progression. There was a head office which administered to ten regions of the country. Each region was then subdivided into a dozen or so districts and each district had up to 20 units. Bill joined the unit nearest to his home.

In a matter of days, he discovered that, as a result of a 'market force' culture in the organisation, there was rivalry between the units to increase productivity. For a few months he enjoyed the challenges but soon found that the ever increasing demands from the district management resulted in a treadmill of procedures and policies that had to be followed. Bill figured that 'if you can't beat them, join them', so he sought openings in his district office. Unfortunately, once tarred with a 'unit' label the doors to 'district' were closed, so were the opportunities at regional level and as for head office, he was told not to think about it. Posts at these other levels were widely advertised and in all cases this was just to show that the organisation operated an open recruitment policy. The bosses had already decided on their internal candidates who would be promoted and the advertisements were just window dressing to keep officialdom happy.

Bill was nothing if not pragmatic, so he decided that he would rise to the top in his unit instead. There were five people above him in the strict pecking order of grades and any promotion would only happen when the top man moved on or dropped dead. Then everyone would move up one place; however, the current head honcho showed no signs of ill health.

Bill had a clear choice. He could just sit back, accept the status quo and follow his immediate supervisor's admonition not to rock the boat or he could leave. Although his academic career had been below average, he had excelled at essay writing at school, so during his lunch breaks he would scribble columns and articles which he would then type out and submit to the trade papers and magazines. To his amazement one of them was accepted for publication—but it was read by his boss and, because it was critical of the organisational structure and had been published under his own name, it was immediately suggested that he should consider his position. This meant that he could tender his resignation or be sacked. He resigned.

He now works from home as a freelance journalist, enjoying the hours that he wants to work, doing what he really enjoys. There is no pecking order, no scramble for promotion and no boss. In a recent radio interview he was asked to look back on his life to see if he had any regrets. 'Only one,' he said. 'I wasted a year of my life in that organisation which, since that time, has gone through many "reorganisations" but their culture hasn't changed one iota as a result. The upside is that because of their attitude it forced me to examine my talents and to put my trust in myself, so I suppose I should thank them for that.'

Do you feel really fed up with your job? Have things been going wrong for you? Have you experienced an awful week or a lousy couple of months? Is your new boss not treating you as you would wish? Have you decided to look for a change in your career or profession?

Hold on before you 'jump ship' and rush off to another job because you could simply be hurrying from one unsuitable working environment to another where you will be doing the same work or else going to the same type of unsuitable company. Stop! Take stock of where you are, who you are, what you love to do, what you are good at doing and how long you want to keep doing it.

There is often a great temptation to react to your current challenges before considering all the avenues that are available to you. Spend a few minutes on the questionnaire below. Your answers will offer insights into your situation and empower you to make better choices.

Spend time considering each line, honestly marking it out of 10. Use 10 for absolutely true, all the way down

> **SELF DIAGNOSTIC BOX**
> **What do I define as a fantastic career for me?**

to 0 if not true. An easy way to complete this task with the necessary degree of honesty is to remember situations or events at work, both positive and negative, and to think of them whilst working through the list. Any numbers **5** or below indicate a degree of dissatisfaction. Put the number in the right-hand column.

Work satisfaction questionnaire	0–10
Your work/job	
I like the people I work with	
My manager provides adequate support for my work	
I like the environment I work in	
My company treats people fairly and ethically including me	
I have control and a direct impact on most of the decisions affecting my work or freedom of choice	
The hours I work suit me	
I am paid at the right level for the responsibilities and requirements of my job	
I am comfortable communicating with my colleagues	

Work satisfaction questionnaire	0–10
I am comfortable communicating with my management	
My colleagues respect my work and appreciate me	
My manager respects my work and appreciates me	
My manager has a reasonable expectation of the goals I can achieve	
I love the type of job I perform	
I know I am in the right career for me	
My job constantly builds on my talents and skills set	
I know I am successful and I am rewarded accordingly	
I feel able to express myself without fear of reprimand	
My job allows me some elements of creativity	
My job fits in well with my personality	
I enjoy my everyday work duties and activities	
My talents are fully utilised in my job	
My job relates directly or has sufficient aspects of my personal interests	
My job brings meaning to my life	
My work and personal life are balanced	
My achievements at work are as I expected them to be	
I am learning and using new skills and talents	
My career choice was selected on my aspirations and needs	
I constantly keep up-to-date with global developments in my career	

If you marked any of the statements in the above questionnaire with 5 or below, you could be experiencing a degree of uneasiness in your job or career. Causes of uneasiness can be varied and can include the influences or impact of any of the following:

- Erratic changes in management
- Poor work environment
- Poor management
- Poor company communications
- Values not in line with company's
- Industry chaos
- Lack of security
- Global influences
- Unsuitable hours
- Negative company culture
- Skills mismatch
- Workload increased
- Burn-out
- Limited opportunities
- Restricted company growth
- Company share price drop
- Salary incorrect
- Too much travel
- Personality mismatch
- Glass ceilings
- Unfulfilled potential
- Lack of company stability
- Redundancies
- New laws/regulations

If any of the above apply to you, put a circle around it and see if there is a pattern or a link between them as this might help with your decision making process.

First things first

The first thing to do before changing your career is to consider the question 'Where am I now?' by defining exactly and honestly all your achievements.

Include skills from your current career and all of your past careers or jobs. Concentrate on those that you have particularly enjoyed doing and the ones where you excelled. You are a unique individual with specific talents, skills and abilities which you have developed during your life, both within your jobs and in your private life. Write a list of everything you can do from the mundane, like ordering the stationery to the more demanding, like five-year financial forecasting. Everything must go down on this list.

I often find that the underlying reason why people are dissatisfied at work is because they have not yet discovered their life purpose and by completing the list you are on your way to discovery.

SELF DIAGNOSTIC BOX

What are my main skills and talents?

Your life purpose

What is your life purpose and how will knowing this make your working life better? Well, once you discover and understand the things that you value highly you can turn them into a life worth living—a life purpose. Most people are content just living their life with little thought about whether it is a good fit with what they could or should do in their own ideal world of personal success.

What is your purpose in life? It is *not* just to make money or to get a job. These things may facilitate your journey towards your life purpose but it is not necessarily your life purpose. When you discover your life purpose and know that it matches your values you will be able to identify what actions and work are right to take you towards your destiny.

Are you the same person at work as you are at home? By changing yourself to fit in with your company's ethics and values you will be leading a double life and putting extra stress and strain on your daily happiness. When you know your life purpose it is easier to take the right decisions when making 'life defining' choices.

You may spend a third of each weekday at work. Today, most of us are no longer prepared to put up with a stressful and false lifestyle. With the acceptance of self-expression through work and with higher expectations for ourselves and others we have changed the way we see an occupation or career. Our world is constantly changing and these changes are happening at breathtaking pace. Consider yourself lucky that you have been born during these exciting times and joyously take advantage of them.

Major career changes are often inflicted by redundancy. The great thing about redundancy is that you get to choose your reaction. You can see it as a disaster and a plague which will ruin your life, or you can see it as a chance to choose a new pathway, a time to decide to take an exciting new career direction, to start with a clean sheet and to redesign your life.

> **SELF DIAGNOSTIC BOX**
>
> **Am I the same person at work as I am at home?**

Redundancy can be the kick up the pants that you need to shake you out of a complacent rut. It can be an opportunity in disguise, forced upon you to offer the greatest rewards as long as you are brave enough to examine all of your options and not just keep on moving along that same old career path.

Your challenge is to avoid being sucked into the 'normal' thought pattern where, because all of your peers are doing something, you believe that it must be the right thing to do. It could be, but the only way to know this for sure is to take the time to analyse what you are doing, what is available to you and what you really would love to do. If, after examining all your options, you decide to follow the herd and do the same old, same old, then good, you are truly happy in your career and you know it.

Take advantage of change

The times are a-changing because of the Internet. This means that people are 'hot-desking', where you no longer have an allocated cosy desk area. Instead, you simply have your desk contents in a box and, when you arrive at work, you collect your box and find a space to work in.

This concept has allowed for employee migration and company savings. It has cut the corporate umbilical cord and, as a result, people no longer feel that they 'belong' to the team or the company. They do the job and go home and this freedom has also freed their minds. The Internet means that people in suitable occupations are able to work from home. There was initial scepticism about home working with managers thinking that 'out of sight equals out of mind' and that the employees would not perform their jobs well. Interestingly, it has often proved the reverse. With no colleague distractions, with clear guidelines and targets coupled with online reporting (your boss knows if you are online and what you are doing) the home worker enjoys greater responsibility, freedom and, perhaps above all, a degree of personal control over their time. For many these are perfect combinations.

In many jobs you are able to choose how you work, where you work and what you do. Because life has changed so dramatically, people are choosing to change their attitude to work and play as well. Employees seek careers which offer balance. The importance of a satisfactory work–life balance, along with these changes of attitudes and aspirations, has given rise to the rewarding profession of life coaching. Again, perfect times, perfect timing and perfect combinations.

What do you really want to do? You can select a career that you love and because you love it you will be good at it and do it lovingly with pride in your achievements. There are hundreds of books on how to choose your career, how to be self-employed and how to run a business. You can even apply for government grants for business start-up and business training.

There are back-to-work schemes for mothers and for the long term unemployed that offer funds and support to help people get work. There are charity grants with free training to help you start your own business. Banks offer interest-free schemes or introductory free periods to support fledgling entrepreneurs. There are organisations such as the Federation of Small Businesses and Business Link that offer support, legal assistance and expertise. It probably has never been as easy to start a business or to change careers without stigma and with encouragement and support. It is commonly reported that the only regret of someone who is going it alone is that they didn't do it sooner.

It is time to return to your life purpose and below there are four tables asking you to consider similar *but* different areas of your life. Once you have completed the four tables it will give you a wider picture of who you are and what you want to happen in your life.

Look at the following table and think about the things you really want from life. Pretend that you are sitting in a wicker rocking chair, aged 93 and looking back on your life as you would have wanted to have lived it. Once you have this mental picture start to fill in the table.

List nine things that you WANT from your life
1.
2.
3.
4.
5.
6.
7.
8.
9.

Now go back to the work satisfaction questionnaire and look at the statements with 6 or more against them. Using these, and anything else that may come to your mind during this activity, identify what is it that makes you special? Remember not to censor your thoughts.

List nine things that make you UNIQUE, SPECIAL or DIFFERENT
1.
2.
3.
4.
5.
6.
7.
8.
9.

Now, including all other areas of your life, consider what you excel at. This is no time for modesty; this is just for you and about you. Remember not to censor your thoughts and be aware that there may be some similar words or phrases from the above two tables, and that is fine.

List nine things that you are GOOD at doing and enjoy doing
1.
2.
3.
4.
5.
6.

7.
8.
9.

Pretend, once again, that you are sitting in a wicker rocking chair, aged 93 and looking back on your life as you would have wanted to have lived it. With this exercise in your mind complete the next table, and remember not to censor your thoughts.

List nine things that you WANT TO HAPPEN or are HELPING TO MAKE HAPPEN in the world
1.
2.
3.
4.
5.
6.
7.
8.
9.

Now look over all your completed tables and highlight words which are similar or the same. Also, mark any words which resonate with you, as these words are important when considering your life purpose. Using some or all of the words you have highlighted, put them together to complete your life purpose statement. This can be a one line sentence or a short paragraph, it does not matter. All that matters with this activity is that you discover your own personalised life purpose—a direction for your life.

If you are struggling you can use the framework below separately, in conjunction with blind choice method (a) or blind choice method (b) on its own. Select your own words to fit the gaps in the statement. Choose words which resonate with you and make you feel absolutely convinced that they create the very best life purpose statement for you. The key here is there are no right or wrong words or statements. If it is right for you, it is right for you.

Using my ...... I will ......, which will bring about ...... and because of this, I will be ......

Here is an example of a life purpose statement that one of my clients created using this technique:

Using my *teaching skills* I will *build a training company specialising in leadership courses*, which will bring about *changes in attitudes towards leadership in business* and because of this, I will be *fulfilled*.

Blind choice methods

This way of creating your life purpose involves you writing the words or phrases you have selected from the tables onto different pieces of paper. Turn the bits of paper upside down on a surface and mix them up until you do not know what is where.

(a) Now pick up a word and put it into the statement above where you feel it best fits. Continue with this until you have words for all the spaces.
(b) Arrange the words or phrases you have turned over into a life purpose you are happy with. You can choose to discard any words you have turned over which do not feel right for you at this stage.

The activity you have just completed is to help you *find* your life purpose statement. You can use any of the words or phrases in your tables to *make* your life purpose statement. You can use the words in any combination and you can also create a completely different styled purpose statement. It does not matter one bit how you do it or if you use the framework above; what is key is that you find your life purpose. You are designing a life purpose statement that reveals your passionately driven destiny and one that will give you the motivation to get out of bed on a frosty morning.

Well done!

Know your natural tendencies

Now you need to consider your personality and the interpersonal skills you have and how this affects your interaction with others who can help you achieve your life purpose.

Extroverts: Do you enjoy interacting with customers and colleagues? Do you like to have a laugh at work? Do you like to have music playing in the background?

Introverts: Do you prefer to work on your own? Do you prefer to work in research? Are you distracted by noise and prefer silence around you? Do you feel uncomfortable dealing with customers? Do you like to rely on your own judgements?

As you can see from these two different groups, it is useful to consider what personality traits you have and feel comfortable with, as they will impact your life and your career. For example, if you enjoy working with people, your next career move should include people contact. Even this people contact should be defined because, if you like working face to face, then becoming a customer relations officer working solely on the telephone will just not do it for you. Yes, the role has customer contact but, and this is important, it does not have the right type of contact that you need for job satisfaction. This job would be fine as a stop-gap position but would not be a good long term career move. The telephone contact would in no way compensate for your need to 'press the flesh' and will eventually cause you unrest. You must be very specific about the aspects of the jobs which you really enjoy and be brutally honest about the things you hate or do not enjoy doing.

People often settle for more things they do not enjoy doing within a job just for the sake of one thing that is important to them. I know people who have settled for working locally instead of having job satisfaction. If you are one of these, do you really need to settle for this?

What does working with people mean to you? Does it mean:

1. Meeting them face to face?
2. Talking over the telephone?
3. Selling within the service industry?
4. Working in an employee support role?
5. A caring capacity—not necessarily medical?
6. Media—in research?
7. Computer training—end-user skills?

I have put together this simple example to show how you can start being specific. Once you have completed this exercise, work out the percentage of time you want to spend on each aspect of the job. What are your current percentages and are you happy with them?

You have already completed a table with nine things that you are good at. Now expand the list to at least 35 things that you are good at doing—whether in your current career, previous jobs, your home, your leisure activities and include anything you are good at, even if it is skipping or knitting. Just put down whatever comes into your mind without censorship. Keep on going, and even when you think you have exhausted the list, add silly things to make the full 35. You must keep on going until you have the full list because often the last few things that come out are the things you have been suppressing and the ones which will make the biggest difference. Have fun with this.

Now give each item on your list a score out of 5, where 0 means you hate doing it and 5 means you love it. Write a new list which includes only the items that you have marked with a 5 or 4. This list of your talents and skills is also a list of things you will excel at because you enjoy doing them.

The X and Y generations know the need for self-expression through work and not simply after work. Most of the baby-boomers live from a mindset of poverty and duty regardless of self. They control themselves from the feeling of lack (self-worth, freedom, food, money, life purpose). People used to believe that they had no power as an individual but now we understand and know this is not true. The internet continues to define and influence the way that we live, interact and have access to information. If you do not currently have computer skills sufficient to use the Internet I strongly urge you to learn.

As you could be spending up to one third of your life at work, ask yourself, 'Is my working life moving me towards my purpose and honouring my values?' Only when the answer to this question is a resounding 'yes' are you on the path to success in your chosen career.

It is critical to know the impact that your core values are having on your life because these heavily influence the way that you make decisions.

There is a step-by-step guided exercise in Chapter Five, Self Success, which helps you to discover your values and put them into an order of importance to you. If you skipped Chapter Five, or you prefer a less structured approach to your activities, you can use this quick alternative technique to discover your values. Ask yourself:

> ## SELF DIAGNOSTIC BOX
>
> ## How am I expressing my purpose and my values in my life right now?

1. What is important to me in life?
2. Can I touch the thing the word describes or is it intangible?

For example, if the first answer is 'Money' then the second answer will be 'Yes'. Money is not a value because you can touch it—the value is what money means to you. Freedom, independence, security and peace of mind are all personal values that can be associated with money.

Simply repeat the questions 'What is important to me in life?' and 'Can I touch the word or is it a value?' several times until you have a list of at least eight to ten core values which are intangible, ethereal and otherwise indefinable as this will help you to ensure the words you have selected really are values.

Now rank your values from the most important to the least important to establish your hierarchy of values. Those at the top of your list will be the most important and you must strive to make your career choices appropriate to these when you are ready to change your job. Similarly, check that any company values align closely to your own.

You will find it much easier to make any life defining decisions once you know your value hierarchy. You will be ready to accept the opportunities and take the options best suited to your life purpose based on what is important to you. When you know your values and you are living congruently with them in both your career and your home life, then you will begin to live a balanced life. A successful life is a balanced life.

Matching values to careers

Perhaps when you were completing the earlier exercises and tables you discovered that your current career is not nourishing either your purpose or values. What do you need to do to live your values and fulfil your purpose?

Write a long list of jobs, careers, industries, businesses or occupations	Against each one on the list, write your values if they are represented
Nurse	Devotion, respect, honesty
Banker	Honesty, respect, security
Business owner	Freedom, challenges, adventure
Plumber	Sense of achievement, resourceful, respect

Take a look at the sample matrix for matching values to work (above), then fill in the table below or copy it into your journal. Remember to leave the censoring behind and just write down as many as you can think of, then add a few more!

Write a long list of jobs, careers, industries, businesses or occupations	Against each one on the list, write your values if they are represented

Highlight the careers/jobs/companies/industries which have the most of your values against them. Well done! Now you have a valuable list of suitable jobs, companies or industries for you to consider.

To make a balance and check you can create a matrix, like the one opposite, as a direct comparison tool. It is an easy method for finding the closest match of work and values. As a result, you are more likely to be living a happy and fulfilled life where at the end of each day you are satisfied with a job well done and, even on a wet Monday morning, you will happily jump out of bed!

Let's have a look at one of my trained coaches. Her purpose in life is 'to support individuals with my coaching skills as they act to achieve their goals'. When she has achieved this, she has fulfilled her values of freedom, love, respect and sense of achievement. She is living her purpose aligned with her values. Because she coaches and charges by the hour, and only the hours she wants or needs to, she has her freedom. By assisting her clients to achieve their goals they all have a genuine sense of achievement. She is respected as a competent coach by her clients and her contemporaries.

How to use this matrix

In the left column write all the criteria you *would like* to find in a job—remember not to censor this list, just go for everything your ideal job/career would have. I have put in some ideas to get you started. Please delete if they are not appropriate to you. Along the top of the matrix put the names of the employers you are interested in working for or careers that interest you. Measure each job criteria against each possible employer/career on a scale of 0 to 10. Use 0 to show not available/offered and use a sliding scale to 10 indicating fully meeting your criteria and your personal requirements.

Please avoid censoring your criteria; just keep on writing regardless, even if you have never heard of a job which includes what you love to do or are good at. Once you run out of ideas go and take a break for 15 minutes and come back to it and write some more things. Once you have exhausted your creativity and thoughts,

Criteria	Company or job				Totals
	Achievement Specialists Limited	Life coaching	Corporate coaching	Business coaching	
Coaching					
Personal development					
Good earning potential					
Matches at least three of my values					

have another break before coming back and putting your criteria list in order of importance to you.

Place the most important (you would not accept a job which did not offer these) at the top of the matrix and the least important (could not care less about this item) at the bottom. Leave all the things on the list because sometimes it is the lower items that are the tipping point for a job. Now that you have all the criteria in order of preference on the matrix, mark the companies or jobs on offer against your list. Select the one with the highest score. Good luck and enjoy the process.

Once you know what careers would suit you, decide if you need to be employed to do this or if it would be better for you to achieve this by being self-employed or owning a business. Make this decision without regard to your financial commitments as this is a decision for the future not about where you are now. Whatever you decide will be right for you.

Now you must compare your current expenditure with your income. Go to Chapter Six, Financial Success, and work through the exercises to give you the information you need. Once you are clear about your financial situation you can make decisions about your future.

As soon as you have all the information concerning your life purpose and values you must make a list of the actions you need to take to achieve these at work. Put these actions in sequential order because some things will only be able to take place once others are completed. A simple example is you may want to be a mobile hairdresser but you have no car and have not passed your driving test. It is simple to work out what comes first and it is the same for your life purpose. It will be easy to identify what needs to be done and in what order.

An irritant at work

So far, this chapter has dealt with considerations that you should include when you are seriously thinking about a career change or a job of a different sort. There are, however, circumstances that are surprisingly common and less extreme. You can be doing a job that you enjoy, that uses your skills and talents, that gives you job satisfaction and yet, you are less than happy and, as you know by now, unhappiness is *not* a feature of success.

Let me give you an example. A competent PA enjoyed her role which, as she put it, was 'to babysit' the senior practice partner that she was assigned to. He never complained but, and this really bugged her, he never gave any praise either. Her peers would enjoy the occasional drink after hours or a birthday cake with their partner directors, but this man seemed to think he was too important to become involved in such trivia.

What started as a minor annoyance for our PA soon became an irritation that diminished the pleasure she derived from her role. She tried broaching the subject with her boss but he dismissed her comments as an emotional reaction, saying that work and leisure should never be mixed. Only when she requested to be moved to another partner, with whom she got on very well, did the original man realise the folly of his ways, especially when he got through five temporary agency PAs in as many months.

Our PA had followed the correct protocol by voicing her concerns to her boss, which was correct, and yet he did nothing. So, as soon as the opportunity arose she jumped sideways and immediately resumed the enjoyment that had attracted her to the role in the first instance. Often in a situation like this the employee can over-react, resign and leave the company instead of looking within the organisation for another suitable role.

If you find your morale slipping in a similar situation, always follow the correct procedures laid down by your employer. Stick to facts and not conjecture. You must never 'go above anyone's head' or 'behind their back'. Avoid spreading discontent with barbed comments or gossip around the coffee machine or photocopier as this always tarnishes your reputation. If you have followed all the rules and the situation remains unchanged, you have three options.

1. You can rise above the issue to grin and bear it, if other aspects of the job still delight you.

2. Wait until a suitable position within the company becomes vacant and apply for it.
3. Otherwise, you can begin considering your future with that company, at which stage you had better go back to the beginning of this chapter and start following its suggestions.

From now on

You know your life purpose and your values. You know the type of career you want and the industry sector that contains your dream career. You will have decided if you want to be employed or self-employed and you are ready to go. Now you must decide to take action and set a date by which you will have done so to move towards your life purpose. The action can be small or large—it can be to buy a book, go on a course, hire a coach or resign—only you know what to do and when to do it. Make a project plan and get going. Remember to enjoy the journey and you will arrive at your destination fresh and happy.

Career success is your privilege and your right. I recently met a client who told me, 'I love my job so much that I would probably do it for fun, even if I wasn't paid for it.' This is surely the ideal. You owe it to yourself not to settle for anything less.

Success Box

1. What would be your dream job?

2. Write the current list of things you are good at

3. Clarify your life purpose

4. Write your core values

5. Design a life project plan

Action I Will Take

Completed on:

/   /

Action I Will Take

Completed on:

/   /

Action I Will Take

Completed on:

/   /

Action I Will Take

Completed on:

/   /

Action I Will Take

Completed on:

/   /

Action I Will Take

Completed on:

/   /

Chapter Thirteen

Entrepreneurial Success

*Unless you were born into an extraordinarily wealthy family,
you will have to earn money to provide clothing, food and shelter.
Most do this by following a vocation, getting a job or building a career.
This chapter is about doing it another way.*

Synopsis

**This chapter tells you how to recognise an entrepreneur at a
thousand paces and how to decide if you are one. It reveals the
pitfalls that can happen to the entrepreneurial free spirit and
offers antidotes to each of them—all except one!**

Lauren Lake sat in the hotel foyer with her journal on her lap.
Although it was only an hour or so after dawn, it was very warm
outside, so she enjoyed the air conditioned comfort as she waited
for the tour bus to arrive for the excursion to Marrakech. On the
first page she wrote, in her small neat hand: 'Tangier is on the
north coast of Morocco, opposite Gibraltar at the entrance to the
Mediterranean. The city has a truly cosmopolitan air where Arab,
African and European cultures appear to exist happily together. It
is this ethnic diversity that attracted me to …'

Then the bus arrived for its final pick-up before embarking on the
long, dusty drive. She boarded with the quick efficiency that gov-
erned most of her movements, put her small bag in the overhead
locker and kept the journal and pen in her hand as the journey
began. It was to be a journey that changed her life.

Now, ten years later, as Lauren took her customary afternoon siesta
in the delightfully restored riad (villa) that she had bought on the
cliff tops above the Medina, she allowed her thoughts to drift back
to that bus trip.

Was it fate that she found herself sitting next to Chuck from Texas on that bus? Was it her sense of adventure that led her to accept his offer? What on earth had possessed her to embark on a venture that even a European man would find difficult, let alone a woman in this country where 'equality' was still an alien concept?

She and Chuck had spent the day together. He explained that he owned a printing firm in Houston and she revealed that she was bored with her job as a legal secretary in Hastings. By the time they shared a large bottle of ice cold Coca Cola beneath the trees at a Marrakech outdoor cafe, she had learned that he had just acquired a printing works in Tangier, with the intention of raising the quality standard, which, until then had been, in his words, 'worse than Russian toilet paper'.

Chuck had to return to the US in a few days' time to take care of business and had little trust in his Moroccan site manager in Tangier. Would she like the job? That was really as much as Lauren could recall of their conversation except that it took her all of five seconds to say 'Yes please'.

Thanks to its high quality output, fair prices and prompt delivery times, which were all novel concepts in Tangier at that time, the print works thrived. Lauren, who was in a self-employed and profit sharing capacity, became wealthy enough over the years to acquire a beauty salon, a holistic health centre and an estate agency.

In each instance she had followed Chuck's original idea of 'find a need, fill it and do it better than all the rest'. He still acted as her mentor although he now rarely ventured outside Houston. 'I am taking the time to enjoy the rewards of all the risks I took,' he said. Lauren still couldn't imagine ever wanting to do something similar because she was having too much fun running her businesses. She was still only 30 anyway and enjoyed taking risks.

I once asked my junior school teacher the meaning of a word. 'Look it up,' she said. Then, a little more gently, 'If I tell you, you will probably forget it by tomorrow. If you look it up, you'll probably remember it all your life.' As we embark on this chapter I can readily identify with her reasoning, except that you could look up dictionary definitions of 'entrepreneur' all day but you would still be no wiser about what makes one, how to recognise one, how to deal with one or how to be a successful one.

Entrepreneurship is even more difficult to define in meaningful terms; in fact, I would probably find it easier to knit spaghetti. Instead I will do what every entrepreneur would be tempted to do. Instead of jumping over or through that particular hoop, I shall just walk around it by describing some of the qualities of entrepreneurs. See how many resonate with you.

1. They dislike being told what to do, but ask politely and they'll do anything for you.
2. Expect to be asked, 'Why?' If you forbid something, they will ask, 'Why not?'
3. When asked a question, they will immediately offer 'Yes' or 'No' but never, ever 'Maybe'.
4. They subscribe to the notion of 'do it now—if not sooner'.
5. They have low thresholds of boredom and seek ways of making any task enjoyable.
6. They are dynamic, enthusiastic, passionate, challenge motivated and determined.
7. They make instant decisions and dislike debates, meetings, reports and committees.
8. They have a highly developed sense of self-worth.
9. They thrive on risk, but only after rapidly weighing up the possible downsides and upsides.
10. They can be aggravating, irritating, annoying and, above all, charming.

If you ticked those that apply to you, then you might become a successful entrepreneur. If you didn't bother, you could almost certainly become one if you wish, because you are keen to see what comes next.

I believe that entrepreneurs are born and not made. I also believe that all of us have the seeds of entrepreneurship within. Some create the opportunities that allow that seed to develop, grow and flourish whilst others simply accept what they are told; they follow convention and the seed dies.

There is another important characteristic. Entrepreneurship is closely related to daydream believing. A dreamer has great ideas and does nothing with them. An entrepreneur may have the same ideas and will act to make something happen. In some ways I should not be writing about success in this context as all entrepreneurs are, in their own minds, already successful. They simply describe any setbacks as being a result of work in progress as they seek their personal 'next big thing'. Entrepreneurs are life's optimists.

They are pragmatists too. The pessimist may see that glass as half empty. The optimist sees it as half full. The entrepreneur sees it as an opportunity to create a better glass or to eliminate its need altogether for it is neither half full nor half empty—it is an exciting challenge.

Paradoxically, it is all their wonderful qualities that can lead to frustration and even depression (entrepreneurs tend to be on a 'high' or a 'low' with no middle ground!). A frustrated entrepreneur may even become a problem employee who is a perpetual

> **SELF DIAGNOSTIC BOX**
>
> Am I an optimist, a pessimist or an entrepreneurial spirit?

misfit. They do not make good team players although they can be inspirational and evangelical team leaders as long as they believe in a cause. If that cause happens to coincide with your company or corporate objectives you have a winner on your staff. Beware if it is at odds, because entrepreneurs can also be self-destructive.

Entrepreneurs cannot be broken down by age and sex. This doesn't mean that they have found the elixir of youth (although many appear to have done so!) but rather that they may be any age, gender, background or nationality. They are found in every town, state, county, country and continent. It is surely beyond coincidence that so many entrepreneurs look younger than their years.

This is possibly where you expect me to list all the usual suspects as examples of entrepreneurship in Britain and the US over the years. If you expected this, you are still not an entrepreneur because we always expect the unexpected. Yes, 'we'. I am an entrepreneur too which is why I know their strengths and weaknesses so well. Instead of listing the great and famous, let's take a closer look at some of those weaknesses and offer their antidotes to enhance your chances of success.

SELF DIAGNOSTIC BOX

Have I ever identified a need and then taken action to fill it?

The curse of the serial entrepreneur

If you turn back the pages of an entrepreneur's story, you will find that their present occupation and preoccupation are probably just the latest in a long line of initiatives. Like the homeowner who looks for a better house just as their first one is becoming debt free, the serial entrepreneur is always striving for something better. Therein may lie the source of a potential danger for just as total success is within their grasp they are likely to tire of that particular business, profession or activity in order to embrace something new and more exciting.

The antidote is to hang on in there with the original concept and run it in tandem with planning that brave new adventure. Entrepreneurs dislike being told to slow down but they are adept at keeping several balls in the air at one time, so if you are having entrepreneurial fun now, you can double it by holding on to its source as you develop the new direction.

The impatience of facing steady progression

Entrepreneurs tend to be 'Type A' personalities who, despite their often voiced claims to be laid back, are capable of amazing bursts of frenetic activity. This tendency can alienate those of a more sedate demeanour who prefer to move from A to B and then progressively to Z whilst the entrepreneur may leap directly from A to Z.

Their impatience can make them seem as if they despise the 'lesser mortals' who they leave in their turbulent wake. However, even entrepreneurs recognise that they need support from other professionals or service providers from time to time and entrepreneurial success comes to those who are able to take time out as they wait for others to play catch-up. If you are guilty of this tendency towards impatience, remember to use these periods to create new ideas or ventures to energise you for when it is time to engage top gear again.

If I can't do it alone, I won't do it at all

This is a destructive trait and is reminiscent of the spoilt child who would rather throw his toys out of the pram than share them with a sibling. The 'urge to go it alone' is a common factor amongst entrepreneurs and it can be the pivotal point of failure.

Entrepreneurs tend not to be joiners of things like clubs, groups, committees or teams (especially teams) as they are instinctive leaders rather than followers. If they do become involved, they can be valuable workers because they are always looking for a more effective or better way to do things and often end up running the organisation.

It was surely an entrepreneur who coined the phrase about 'working smarter rather than harder' although they are anything but work-shy either. Entrepreneurial success means knowing others may have the answers, being prepared to ask them for the answers and then accepting any help when it is offered. Some events will take as long as they take, no matter how you may fret and fume at apparent delays and the time taken to deliver high quality workmanship.

The considerate but annoying escort

Entrepreneurs tend to make exciting partners in a social context and if you cohabit with one you will never be bored as long as you remember to expect the unexpected.

Take an entrepreneur to the theatre and they may well miss most of the first act of the play while they mentally redesign the programme notes, the scenery, the seating and even the location of the refreshment kiosk. They are not being discourteous or ungrateful; it is just the way that their entrepreneurial mind works.

Take them to an outdoor event and you can expect to find your escort in deep conversation with the owners of the various exhibition or concession stands. They will be intrigued to know why the owners are there, is it profitable and whether they have the same pitch every year. This is an urge to be part of the action because it is alien to the entrepreneurial nature to be a non-participating spectator.

> **SELF DIAGNOSTIC BOX**
>
> Have you been to an event you knew you could organise far more efficiently?

Frankly, there is no antidote to this characteristic. It probably doesn't matter though because your dynamic subject will have totally forgotten all about the event by the next day as he or she flits on to the next interesting event just waiting to be improved.

Getting an adrenalin rush from a risk

To misquote a proverb: Entrepreneurs rush in where angels fear to tread! Although many will deny it, an entrepreneurial personality will delight in taking, apparently, the most outrageous risks, saying that they 'enjoy the thrill'. This may not be strictly truthful because, in their own minds, they will have assessed every aspect of the risk at the speed of light, depending heavily on their intuition and gut instincts. Fortunately they tend to be right and survive to live another day or three.

The biggest risk taken by every entrepreneur actually happens on a daily basis. Unlike people who have a steady job, vocation or career, the entrepreneur may well wake up each morning not just self-employed but self-unemployed. They have to use their guile, charm, talents and skills to create an income as they 'will' the letter to arrive or the phone to ring with a lucrative offer. Without venturing into the fields of the Laws of Attraction or Creative Visualisation, it seems to work for them more often than not.

If you recognise yourself or your partner in this high risk category, do all that you can to ensure that at least your home is safely and financially ring-fenced. Entrepreneurs will baulk at this suggestion as they heartily eschew the concepts of safety nets of any kind. The cruel truth is that even entrepreneurial free spirits need a base for their operations.

The entrepreneur as an employee

Entrepreneurs between projects can often turn up in the most unlikely jobs where they will either be outstandingly successful star performers or will move on very quickly.

Their persuasive charm has been known to deceive even case hardened recruitment staff and interviewers, for entrepreneurs are masters of rapport, at least in the short term. They will quickly become bored with routine and if you offer a Company Procedures Manual on the first day you will probably find it, within the first hour, propping up that wonky table leg in the staff kitchen that you had been meaning to fix for months.

Your entrepreneurial employees will be action centred with maverick attitudes. They have little patience with protocol, rank, pecking orders or house rules which they perceive as needless and pointless. They will stray beyond the confines of their own department and responsibilities, especially if they feel restricted by them. They need constant mental stimulation and physical action and if you (or their job description) fail to provide it, they will create their own. They will never be deliberately disruptive or destructive owing to their innate leadership qualities; however, they may, inadvertently create festering unrest amongst their peers and colleagues.

You are unlikely to find an entrepreneur in a strictly career structured occupation nor one where ordered regimentation is present. If you find one as your employee, take consolation from the fact that your involvement will probably be brief and that they will almost certainly come up with some spectacular ideas during their tenure. And that is surely a success gain worth the short-term pain.

Other considerations on entrepreneurship

There are many books and ideas on what makes an entrepreneur and what entrepreneurs should do in order to be successful and I recommend you regularly read books on all aspects of business from start-up to selling your business. Two top contenders for the reasons why people start on the journey of the entrepreneur are:

1. The experienced worker who has decided to set up a business that will grow sufficiently to provide an income to cover the outgoings and add a moderate amount of extra income for luxuries while at the same time giving freedom to make their own decisions.
2. The dynamic thrusting individual who wants to earn 'lots of money' or 'become a major player' or someone who is 'Respected!' and may or may not be passionate about the type of business that generates the money. They are often driven by the need to succeed regardless of the route to success.

Without a good start-up team, your business will stay small but that is not necessarily the end of the world. You will at least have covered all viewpoints before you waste time, money, passion and enthusiasm setting up the wrong framework for your business vision. The key here is that you need the right support systems and mastermind team (mentors, businesses partners, suppliers, etc.) working with you towards the same vision and goals. Your success will come to you because you have the right people with the right skills on your side, which should enable you to avoid most of the normal pitfalls and mistakes other entrepreneurs have made before you. Take Richard Branson as an example of an entrepreneur who faced many enormous barriers and challenges to his success and yet with the right team players and mastermind teams he has forged an enviable global business empire.

The environment of the entrepreneur

What surrounds you will have an impact on you, so surround yourself with an appropriate environment. If you work out of a dirty, dingy back office you are not stimulating your mind. If that is all you can afford, clean it, paint the walls and decorate it with plants and inspirational pictures or quotes. Fix a board on the wall and affix colour pictures, symbols and drawings which represent your future business goal; this is known as a vision board and the principle has been used for many years by successful people. The vision board should stimulate you, bring a huge smile to your face when you look at it and motivate you to achieve. The vision board should be able to boost your enthusiasm during the times you are challenged. It is a constant reminder of where you are going and what you are creating.

Start creating the environment you see yourself working in right at the start of your journey. You can surround yourself with beautiful things—begin by purchasing a beautiful object and placing it in a prominent position where it can inspire you to achieve your goals. Use inspirational accelerators such as your vision board and your success team to create and build your very own environment of success.

So you want to be an entrepreneur?

I am not sure how to break this news to you, so I suppose I must be quick and cruel to be kind. If you think you can become an entrepreneur just by reading a book, you don't have what it takes. There, I have said it!

To repeat the words of Chuck from our opening story: 'Find a need, fill it and do it better than all the rest.' If that prospect excites you, then you may have what it takes. If it doesn't, then forget about it and get a proper job. You may never become seriously rich and yet you may still meet your initial criterion of success. For the true entrepreneur, riches are just a by-product. The chases, the risks, the desire to make a positive difference and to have fun are the elements that float their boat. For an entrepreneur, there are no limits, no rules and no excuses. If you think you are up to it, then welcome to the club. Do your own thing and, like Chuck, enjoy the journey wherever it may lead you and the rewards whatever they may be.

Success Box

1. How many entrepreneurial qualities do you have now?

2. When did you last think 'There must be a better way?'

3. What did you do about it then and what could you do about it now?

4. What is your business vision?

5. What need could you fill now, better than all the rest and without limits or rules?

Action I Will Take

Completed on:

/   /

Action I Will Take

Completed on:

/   /

Action I Will Take

Completed on:

/   /

Action I Will Take

Completed on:

/   /

Action I Will Take

Completed on:

/   /

Action I Will Take

Completed on:

/   /

Chapter Fourteen

Beyond Success

So you have achieved success. Please heed these three warnings
and final suggestions.

Synopsis

Success can corrupt so take the necessary precautions to ensure
that success in your chosen field does not lead to your failure as
a decent human being.

The advance publicity had been expensive and was skilfully exe-
cuted. This, along with the speaker's long reputation, had ensured
that the seminar was a complete 'house full' event.

The star attraction, one of the world's most famous and successful
motivational speakers, was now getting older and was no longer
willing to do a full eight hour presentation so, for the last few engagements he hired Robin, who was a local speaker, to perform for the first
half of the day. When asked whether he feared this competition he
drawled dismissively, 'Of course not! There is no serious competition
anyway! And what the heck, if he bores the pants off 'em they'll drift
out into the foyer and buy more of my books and audio programmes.
They may even sign up for my workshops in the Caribbean ... not
that I'll be there, but they'll have my name on them.'

At that point, the reporter who had asked the question decided that
she would write a less than glowing review for her newspaper.

The star, conscious of all the nuances of show business, had heeded
his publicist and stayed in the dressing room during the comfort
breaks and at lunchtime to avoid 'cheapening the image'. In contrast, Robin the 'support act' made himself freely available and
mingled with the delighted audience at appropriate times.

The after-show queue split into two. The smaller group headed for the great man, eager to get his autograph on the expensive merchandise they had bought. The reporter noted that, although his mouth smiled as he scribbled illegibly on their purchases, the star's eyes had about as much warmth as those of a dead cod. She moved over to the other side of the stage to see why the queue was so much longer. Here, Robin was laughing and joking with his public; he was enjoying himself because they were enjoying him. He had established a fantastic rapport and treated every delegate as an equal. The next day's press reviews were mixed. The star had failed to live up to his hype, but the supporting speaker was a true headliner in the making.

This happened years ago. The once millionaire star turn has now lost most of his wealth in a messy divorce, he hasn't bothered to write any more books and, because his publishers are simply recycling old material in new covers, his sales are plummeting. Robin? Well, he is still pulling in the crowds whenever he appears, he is still happy and he still 'walks his talk'.

Over a cafe table the reporter, now retired, confided: 'The reason for the big man's decline and fall is that he achieved success too early and forgot to be nice. The other guy started humble, remained nice throughout and is now enjoying true success and happiness as a result. It's like the old proverb says, "It is nice to be important, but even more important to be nice".'

This chapter is vitally important. When you absorb the information in this book and then add your own actions and experience, you will convert it into knowledge that allows you to achieve success in reaching your goals, just as thousands of others do around the world, every day.

But that is not the end of your responsibilities. It is just the beginning! I sometimes feel that success should come with warnings.

'That's it then' syndrome

You have planned your success in your chosen area, you have acted to make it happen and the results have been delivered—

what then? It is normal to take a deep breath and a few days of relaxation to enjoy what you have achieved; then there will be a void where your diligence and effort used to be.

Your quest for success can be a habit that is hard to break, so you may well seek to fill this void by moving on to even greater success in the same or another area. That is wonderful if it happens. You will have no initial inertia to overcome, your enthusiasm and energy levels will already be high and your tasks will seem easier than they were the first time around, simply because you have already proven that you *can* do whatever you approach with positive intent.

The downside is that some people allow themselves to drift into a worst case scenario where those few days of relaxation merge into a few weeks and momentum erodes to nothing. There is a sense of anticlimax and that can lead to boredom. There may even be a sense of disappointment when you discover, too late, that the fruits of your success are not as sweet as you imagined they would be. Some successful people become bitter and dispirited and this can create negative moods. You have become a victim of the 'That's it then' syndrome!

> **SELF DIAGNOSTIC BOX**
>
> **Will I suffer from 'That's it then' syndrome?**

As you should expect by now, I have the antidote. Here is a quick checklist that can save you from this anticlimactic ennui or break you out of it if you are already there.

1. At an early stage, plan for what you will do with your new found success.
2. Establish a measure so that you will know when you have achieved it.
3. Sketch in and prioritise three more areas for your next success mission.

4. Set a date for starting work with focus on your first priority 'next big thing'.
5. Follow the suggestions elsewhere in this book to achieve it.
6. Take positive action, one step at a time.

Although I usually recommend that you should never look back, you may find it useful to reflect on *why* you sought your original success. This brief trip back to basics can often provide clues and allow you to make some small, but vital, course adjustments. It is normal for reasons, desires and hopes to change over a period of time as your life, career, business or interests have moved forward.

The bottom line here is that success is a journey, it is not a destination.

Avoid becoming an APE

This is not a criticism of our closest animal relatives and simian friends. Indeed, I have met some apes that have nicer demeanours than some successful humans.

This second warning is about Arrogance, Pride and Ego—or APE.

I am sure that you have encountered a few people who have achieved phenomenal success and have become phenomenally obnoxious people. Yes, of course you should take pride in your significant achievements; but if you display your pride to the world at large you will find that it may well lead to a fall. Just think how the tabloid media loves to build up a hero or iconic figure and then, to boost circulation, assassinates those same celebrities' characters. You have been warned.

Arrogance is never, ever acceptable under any circumstances or conditions. Check your conduct regularly and, if you detect even the faintest whiff of arrogance, take the mental equivalent of a cold shower or a visit to a chemical decontamination chamber. Beware that you do not swing your behaviour pendulum too far in the opposite direction, because excessive or false humility can be perceived as arrogance too.

As for ego, well we all have one. It would be a pretty boring world if everyone was a clone—ego is an integral part of your personality and is what makes you different. The caution here concerns inflated ego, which like a balloon or tyre that is overinflated, can explode in your face with disastrous consequences.

Ask yourself these two questions:

1. Do I light up a room with my presence when I enter it or when I leave it?
2. What do I imagine others say about me when I have left the room?

> **SELF DIAGNOSTIC BOX**
> A, P or E? Which of these is the greatest danger in my life right now?

If the answers are not what you want them to be, then the antidote is to consciously put other people first and engage your brain before you put your mouth in gear. Then you will never become an APE.

Stardom is built on the back of supporting players

A leading actor who was knighted for 'services to entertainment' once told me, 'Be nice to those who help you up that ladder of success, for you never know when you might meet them on your way down.'

Stardom or success is created by you; however, you cannot and did not create it alone. Your support team may have included parents, siblings, spouses, teachers, tutors, peers, superiors, subordinates and total strangers. No matter how small their input may have seemed at the time, it undeniably contributed to where you are now.

As you reach your dizzy heights of success, never look down on others and always treat them as equals. Do not judge other people, especially the ones who were part of your support team because, like you, they are doing the best that they can with the tools, talents, experiences and knowledge that they have. They may even have achieved a greater success than yours in a field about which you are totally ignorant. The checkout girl at the supermarket till may be funding her way through university where, after gaining a first with honours, she is now study-

> **SELF DIAGNOSTIC BOX**
>
> **Has success made me a nicer person to be with?**

ing for her PhD, or she could be caring for a disabled family member. There are some people who would judge that self-sacrifice as the highest form of success.

I usually keep jokes out of my books because humour is such a personal matter of taste. Here I feel I can make an exception. An internationally famous author was at a book signing event in an equally famous Knightsbridge store. A young shop assistant was in his way and, as he pushed her rudely aside he snarled, 'Do you know who I am?' As the girl blushed in confusion, a very elderly lady in a wheelchair tugged at his sleeve: 'Matron is standing over there; just ask her and she will remind you. If she can't remember she'll look at the label inside your coat and tell you from that.'

Spread your gratitude freely

The concept of tithing is as old as history itself. It is the means by which a farmer would donate a percentage of his corn or other harvest to a collective winter grain store. He wouldn't miss it as he probably had more than he could use or sell at the end of the season and he would have a right to draw from the store in lean times.

The practice was then extended to other areas, where a landlord, lord of the manor, duke, earl, baron or lesser king would extract a cash tithe from his subjects. Then a few religions caught on to the idea and replaced the collecting plate with a compulsory donation. Governments, who have always known a good idea when they see it, jumped on to the bandwagon too, but they call it taxation.

It has sometimes been suggested that an obsession with success is simply a slippery slope to selfishness. It can be, but it can equally be a wonderful opportunity for selflessness. If your success releases some time, you can give your extra time to others who may need it. If it creates wealth, then you can share this too.

I am *not* advocating that you give out of a sense of duty, that you give with strings attached, that you boost your ego by massive charity donations or that you give without direction.

Here are five simple rules you can use when giving:

1. Give with no expectation of any personal return or gain.
2. Give anonymously and privately.
3. Give to the sources of your help and inspiration.
4. Give thanks.
5. Give within your means.

Rule 3 can do with a little expanding. If, like me, you have had a close encounter with cancer, then your giving could be towards a cancer research charity. My husband enjoys messing about in boats, so the Royal National Lifeboat Institution is an appropriate recipient for his giving. If you gained spiritual inspiration and support from a synagogue, church, mosque or new age commune, then give back to a synagogue, church, mosque or new age commune. If you gained time for your success because you used a child minder or nursery, then give to a children's organisation.

You should have understood the point by now. Give appropriately. The amount is up to you, of course, however a typical tithe would have been set at around ten per cent because this amount should not compromise your needs for clothing, shelter and food but is significant enough to make a difference elsewhere. Why not consider ten per cent of the *additional* time, money or other resources that your success has delivered. Another benefit is that ten per cent is much easier to calculate for the mathematically challenged!

Karma means that what goes around comes around. The first Christians were told, 'As you give, so shall you receive', which is a neat place to bring this book to a close with a final reminder:

Success is not always measured in purely materialistic terms.

SELF DIAGNOSTIC BOX

What will I give, to whom, how and when?

Success Box

1. Use the suggestions in this book

2. Refer to it often

3. Buy copies as gifts for your friends

4. Enjoy your success

5. Send me your personal success stories

Action I Will Take

Completed on:

/   /

Action I Will Take

Completed on:

/   /

Action I Will Take

Completed on:

/   /

Action I Will Take

Completed on:

/   /

Action I Will Take

Completed on:

/   /

Action I Will Take

Completed on:

/   /

Epilogue: Over to You

Now you need to decide what comes next and how you can keep up your momentum.

When you travel to a town or country for the first time, you will probably use maps and/or satellite navigation devices and then as you near your destination you will be looking out for specific signposts.

When you apply the suggestions in this book you are well on your way to your destination of Personal Success but, because every route is unique, I cannot build the road for you. Instead, in this book, I have provided you with a series of signposts that I have been defining, refining and validating over many years of research and experience.

You always have the luxury of choice. As long as you keep your ultimate outcome in mind and act accordingly, you can choose to follow the signposts or take a diversion along some interesting byways, both of which may offer you very useful insights and tantalising discoveries along the way. The chapters in this book will bring you back on track if you have strayed too far from your life purpose journey.

You may discover that your quest for even greater success is a journey without end, proving that the journey itself may be the destination, leading always to new challenges and experiences to fuel your progress, even if you decide to travel to a totally different place along the way.

In these pages, I have offered you a great deal of information. It is only when you use it and then apply your personal experiences that it is transformed into knowledge. Information may be forgotten in time, but knowledge is with you for ever.

To paraphrase a quotation from Britain's wartime prime minister, Winston Churchill, 'It is not the beginning of the end. It is not even the end of the beginning.' So, although you have now come to the end of this book, you need not continue alone because I have prepared a series of resources to use as your travel companion whenever you are ready.

A great place to begin exploring these resources is the website of my company Achievement Specialists Limited. You can find it at www.achievementspecialists.co.uk and be sure to take a look at the range of coaching services there, which include one-to-one offers, group coaching and business coaching. While you are on the web pages, check out our multimedia coach training courses and explore details of my books, CDs and business networking support services too. If you sign up for my free monthly newsletter, you will discover hints and tips on life coaching, stories to inspire you and also you will be given advance information of new products and services as they become available. You will have access to some special offers and, yes, I'll even share my scheduled TV and radio appearances as well.

If you don't have Internet access yet, you can telephone for more information (from the UK) on free phone 0800 191 0200 or you may write to me personally via Crown House Publishing.

I would love to hear stories of your own personal success and, who knows, they may even become a success feature in my next book or the monthly newsletter.

Thank you for sharing your time with me and I leave you with the thought that I have created my own successful organisation from scratch using the information that you have just read. This fact gives me the final four words of this epilogue. They are:

'I have—you can!'

Author Resource Guide

If you would like to contact Curly Martin, you can do so through the publisher or directly using the contact details below. If you visit the website you will find an abundant resource. There will be programmes and items to keep you on track as you take your success to the next level. Visit now and take advantage of all there is on offer.

E-mail: curly@achievementspecialists.co.uk
Website: www.achievementspecialists.co.uk
                www.curlymartin.com
Free phone: 0800 191 0200

Curly welcomes discussions and is happy to answer any questions you may have about the book or website.

To post your letter to Curly, you may do so via Crown House Publishing Ltd:

> Crown House Publishing
> Crown Buildings
> Bancyfelin
> Carmarthen
> SA33 5ND

Testimonials for Curly Martin

'Curly, your skills, knowledge and wisdom have changed and transformed my world. I thank you for all your guidance this past year and your love for making a difference to so many lives. You are a star!'   K. Cottam

'No words could express my gratitude firstly, for your book that opened the door for me and so many others and for your gift of magic that you have poured on us all. To live in this new place is indescribable. It carries with it a sense of dignity and ease that I have never ever envisaged. From my heart I thank God for it and I thank you also Curly.'   M. Burke

'Absolutely unforgettable – far exceeded my expectations! I now know I chose the right course from the many I looked at. I love your approach, I fee like I've learnt more in this weekend than 5 years of university!! You're brilliant!!'   S. Carver

'Dear Curly, It was a real pleasure to meet you. As I mentioned, your energy is amazing and you really inspire. I thoroughly enjoyed the course, in fact the best personal development course I've been on. I learnt a lot about myself even though I was doing things outside my comfort zone, I felt real warmth, support and encouragement from everyone and the feedback was always very constructive and helpful, in terms of improving in the future. Thanks again for a fun and very inspiring weekend!'   J. Puczkowski

'I just wanted to say thank you so much – it was truly a life changing experience. I burst into tears of utter joy this morning as I was dancing my bum off around the kitchen to Heather Small singing 'Proud'. Being a verbose individual, I could go on and on about it all but I'm not going to. What I'm going to do is get my 'arris into gear and get on with it! Thank you again, Curly.'   M. Phelps

'A supremely powerful learning experience – more than exceeded my expectations. Jam-packed with useful information and practical advice. I highly recommend this opportunity to anyone wanting to enhance their own personal life and business and management skills. You will thoroughly enjoy, and benefit from this unique experience. I am positive that you will come out of this two-day event with the belief that absolutely anything you chose, and dare to dream, is within your grasp.'   T. Palmer

'It has now been over 2 weeks since I participated on your brilliant Life course. Thank you so much for a great course, practical and thought provoking. And wow! I have achieved loads in the last 2 weeks. I am so focussed and results driven – and this is in all aspects of my life, we are eating better; I am keeping fit, I have completed tasks that I have been procrastinating for weeks; (including my tax return); and I feel good (in a James Brown style!) Thank you Curly – you are an inspiration. Warmest Regards.' L. Reed

'LOVED EVERYTHING! Thank you Curly, you are truly an inspiration. This has given me the confidence to be the best person that I can be.' C. Gerro

'Just wanted to say thank you for a great weekend. I was very impressed. As you know I taught in colleges for 8 years and have been to many talks, conferences, trainings, etc. Yours would have to be No 1 – I learnt so much. You kept my attention. Timings were excellent and you delivered what you said you would. Thanks.' G. Crossley

'Awesome! Thank you so much for a fabulous training experience that has left me inspired, enabled and excited.' V. Smith

'Hi Curly, Since I started working with you I have doubled the profit I wanted to achieve. My first goal was for 3 months and my 2nd for 6. I have achieved my 6 month goal Curly! Unbelievable! It has only been 1 month!' N. Roscoe, 'Lifestyle Designer' at Fabulous Lifestyles

'Weekend was fantastic, you have inspired me and motivated me to go ahead with my goals. Best course I have been on in my life. Huge Thanks' S. Wheelan

'I have thoroughly enjoyed the whole weekend. It was great to step out of my comfort zone and make the most of the challenges presented to us. My goal for the two days was to mark the start of my training with a completely focussed couple of days with no distractions – this goal was achieved and exceeded. Thank you – I CAN DO!!' K. Harper

'Excellent in every way I have not excuses to be negative again. Will definitely recommend to anyone who is interested'. J. Colvin

'Dear Curly, THANK YOU SO MUCH for such a fabulous weekend, you are a true inspiration! Like many of us, I've hit a real crossroads in my life, and now I can see the way ahead and I'm so excited! With fond love.' H. Brown

Index